MASTERPIECES
OF THE
BIBLE

MASTERPIECES
OF THE
BIBLE

INSIGHTS INTO CLASSICAL ART OF FAITH

KEITH J. WHITE

BAKER
A DIVISION OF
Baker Book House Co

Published in North America by Baker Books
a division of Baker Book House Company
P.O. Box 6287, Grand Rapids, MI 49516-6287

Printed in Hong Kong

ISBN 0-8010-1151-5

A CIP record for this book is available from
the Library of Congress.

Designed and produced by Tony Cantale Graphics.

For current information about all releases
from Baker Book House, visit our web site:
http://www.bakerbooks.com

Picture Acknowledgments

Pictures supplied by:
The Art Gallery of New South Wales, Sydney: page 35;
Cordon Art B.V., Holland: page 21;
The Bridgeman Art Library: pages 13, 15, 17, 23, 31, 33,
    37, 41, 45, 47, 61, 63, 67, 75, 77, 79, 85, 87, 89, 93;
The British Library, London: page 19
The Metropolitan Museum of Art, New York: pages 55,
    57, 73;
National Gallery, London: front cover, pages 3, 25, 27, 29,
    49, 51, 53, 65, 69, 71, 81, 83;
Scala Picture Library, Milan: pages 39, 59;
Tate Gallery, London: page 91.

p. 21: M.C. Escher's Tower of Babel © 1997 Cordon Art – Baarn –
    Holland. Used with permission.
p. 33: Holman Hunt's The Scapegoat: reproduced with permission
    of Lady Lever Art Gallery.
p. 55: G. de la Tour's The Penitent Magdalen: The Metropolitan
    Museum of Art, Gift of Mr. and Mrs. Charles Wrightsman,
    1978. (1978.517)
p. 57: E. Delacroix's Christ on the Lake of Gennesaret: The
    Metropolitan Museum of Art, Bequest of Mrs. H.O. Havemeyer,
    1929. The H.O. Havemeyer Collection. (29.100.131)
p. 73: Mattia Preti's Pilate Washing his Hands:
    The Metropolitan Museum of Art, Purchase, Gift of J. Pierpont
    Morgan and Bequest of Helena W. Charlton, by exchange,
    Gwynne Andrews, Marquand, and Rogers Funds, Victor
    Wilbour Memorial Fund, The Alfred N. Punnett Endowment
    fund, and funds from various donors, 1978. (1978.402)
p. 87: Holman Hunt's The Light of the World: reproduced by
    permission of the Warden and Fellows of Keble College, Oxford.
p. 93: Graham Sutherland's Christ in Glory in the Tetramorph
    © 1997 Coventry Cathedral. Used with permission.

Masterpieces of the Bible
Contents

		Page
Introduction		7
Old Testament		11
'The Ancient of Days'	William Blake	12
The Creation of Adam	Michelangelo	14
Expulsion from Paradise	Masaccio	16
The Exile from the Ark and the Drunkenness of Noah	Bedford Book of Hours	18
Tower of Babel	Escher	20
Lot Fleeing with His Daughters from Sodom	Dürer	22
Rebecca at the Well	Pellegrini	24
Jacob with the Flock of Laban	Jusepe de Ribera	26
Joseph in Egypt	Jacopa da Pontormo	28
The Brazen Serpent	Tiepolo	30
The Scapegoat	Holman Hunt	32
The Visit of the Queen of Sheba to King Solomon	E.J. Poynter	34
Vision of Ezekiel	Raphael	36
The Three Men in the Fiery Furnace	Catacomb, Rome	38
Belshazzar's Feast	Rembrandt	40
New Testament		43
The Madonna del Granduca	Raphael	44
Christ in the House of his Parents	Millais	46
Christ among the Doctors	Bernardino Luini	48
The Baptism of Christ	Piero della Francesca	50
The Marriage at Cana	Mattia Preti	52
The Penitent Magdalen	Georges de la Tour	54
Christ on the Lake of Gennesaret	Delacroix	56
The Transfiguration	Raphael	58
Kitchen Scene with Christ in the Home of Martha and Mary	Velazquez	60
A Parable: Return of the Prodigal Son	Rembrandt	62
Christ Driving the Traders from the Temple	El Greco	64
The Last Supper	Leonardo da Vinci	66
The Agony in the Garden	El Greco	68
Christ before the High Priest	Honthorst	70
Pilate Washing his Hands	Mattia Preti	72
The Crucifixion	Grünewald	74
Pietà	Michelangelo	76
The Resurrection of Christ	Piero della Francesca	78
Noli Me Tangere (Don't Touch Me)	Titian	80
The Supper at Emmaus	Caravaggio	82
The Conversion of Saul	Michelangelo	84
The Light of the World	Holman Hunt	86
The Four Horsemen of the Apocalypse	Dürer	88
The Great Day of His Wrath	John Martin	90
Christ in Glory in the Tetramorph	Graham Sutherland	92
Bible References to the Pictures		95
Author's Acknowledgements		96

Introduction

THE PURPOSE of this book is to make possible an encounter with stories and events of the Bible through the eyes of artists. 40 pictures have been chosen and arranged in narrative order conforming to their source references in Scripture. They have been selected from many thousands of pictures, some because they are universally acknowledged as masterpieces; others to provide contrasting approaches and styles. The earliest painting is from the third century, the latest is 20th century. They include canvasses, frescoes, altar-pieces, murals and frescoes, a book illustration, a tapestry and woodcuts, of very different sizes and designed for completely different settings and purposes. This variety helps to demonstrate the many ways in which art has been used to illuminate and portray the Bible stories.

There is no one way of encapsulating the truth or meaning of an event. We can only listen to the story in our own language, time and context given the bias of our own life-story and upbringing. The very different styles and approaches of the works reproduced here are examples of this process. The images immediately convey some of the preconceptions and conventions of the artists. We may feel more at home with some than others. Yet if we pause to reflect on alternative approaches aspects of truth and meaning that were previously hidden to us may be revealed. Some pictures here may prove a barrier to such discoveries because the style is so foreign or difficult. If so, we can always move on to the next.

The organisation of the book is as simple as possible. Each picture is ordered under Old or New Testament and accompanied by three brief sections of commentary. The first sets out a few salient details about the artist and the painting. The second gives biblical background information, usually summarising the story or event portrayed. The third is a personal reflection on the painting. The first two sections are designed to enhance the quality of reflection and understanding.

In piloting the book we have found one of the most successful ways of using it is to have two people looking at it together. One reads the reflection while the other is free to study the picture. It is rather like standing in front of a painting in a gallery with a friend, or with a recorded commentary. In an ideal world we could stand together in front of (or underneath) each picture in turn and discuss it together. This book seeks to recreate that sort of encounter and conversation. A problem of course is that I can't gauge your reactions, hear your comments or your questions. For this reason I've sent the text to a number of people of different ages and backgrounds. In the light of their comments it has been extensively revised. The commentary is not intended to be authoritative or didactic, but to provide a starting-point for conversation. Some parts will no doubt prove more effective in this than others. If at any point the words prove a barrier or problem please focus attention on the picture. Words can often get in the way of truth and revelation.

Taken together the pictures provide an outline of much of the biblical story. There is a wealth of material of Jesus and less on the Old Testament stories. This reflects the overwhelming popularity of Jesus as a subject for artists (or their patrons) for many centuries. The narrative begins with the creation of the universe, Adam, and the expulsion of Adam and Eve from the Garden of Eden. There is the Flood, the Tower of Babel, the destruction of Sodom and Gomorrah and incidents in the lives of Isaac, Jacob, Joseph, Moses and Solomon. The Old Testament section concludes with the vision of Ezekiel, the fiery furnace and Belshazzar's Feast. The New Testament section begins with the birth of Jesus, tracing his boyhood, baptism, ministry, encounters right though to the crucifixion and resurrection. The conversion of Saul precedes portrayals of the end of time and the last judgement. It is not an accurate summary of the whole biblical narrative but rather a broad sweep. There is much that is dramatic and challenging, but there is also a gentler, tender strain running through, typified by Rebecca, Jacob, the home of Martha and Mary and the encounter between Jesus and Mary Magdelene.

For some this book may be the first encounter with many of the paintings, and it is my hope that it will open up a whole new way of seeing things. There is no substitute for seeing the works of art themselves and perhaps this will be the beginning of an adventure. I myself have not seen all the originals and still long to search them out. Others may be interested in art and find the narrative organisation of the pictures rather novel. My hope in this case is that something of the mystery and awe at the heart of the biblical stories may be encountered in a new way. You will not find here any great insights into technique or art history, but new relationships and themes may emerge from the juxtaposition of these particular pictures.

Some will be acutely aware of gaps and imbalances in the selection. There are outstanding artists who are not represented at all; there are no works by women or from outside Europe; there is little modern art; dominant biblical characters like David and Isaiah are omitted, and so on. Some such gaps are inevitable in a collection like this. For the record some of the pictures are not my personal preferences and I have found it an illuminating discipline attuning my mind to perspectives and conventions which are far from second nature.

The relationship between painting and the Christian faith has been at times strained and at other times relaxed. At one extreme has been the view that all images of a religious nature should be forbidden because of the commandment not to make any graven images or idols. It was particularly strong in many Protestant denominations after the Reformation. At the other end of the spectrum are those who see such images as holy, as mysterious reflections (or icons) of the supernatural world. This tradition has continued to the present day, notably in the Eastern Church. A pragmatic view was enunciated by Pope Gregory: "Painting can do for the illiterate what writing does for those who can read."

In the course of preparing this book aspects of each view have proved insightful. The book is centered on the biblical narrative and so seeks those illustrations which serve to increase our understanding of the stories or events. At times it has become apparent that an artist is using a picture to demonstrate his own skill or virtuosity. The simplicity of the catacomb painting of the fiery furnace is a useful corrective here. It was not painted as a beautiful thing in its own right (art for art's sake), but to remind believers of God's mercy and power. Any human endeavour can become idolatrous in drawing attention away from the proper focus of our worship and affection. The visual arts are perhaps particularly susceptible to this temptation.

On the other hand if the world is created by God and reflects his handiwork how can anything be ruled out as a potential vehicle for the expression of the divine? Nothing (save Jesus) will be divine in its fulness, but everything may have something of the Eternal in it. Some of the works in this collection have been an extremely powerful means of conveying a sense of God's presence and love. Had they been forbidden or destroyed, our worship, devotion and perhaps even theology might have been the poorer for it.

There is, of course, something in what Pope Gregory said, but there is more to it than that. Logically he implies that if a person can read art is redundant! There are times when the written word is necessary; at other times silence, music, painting, drama will be more appropriate ways of conveying an emotion or an insight. There are aspects of these paintings that cannot be reduced to words, just as there are aspects of the bible story that cannot be reduced to visual images.

One distinction to be kept in mind is that of the public and private. Roman Catholic and

Orthodox places of worship are typically adorned with paintings, frescoes, sculptures and the like, while many Protestant churches and chapels are deliberately bare save for an elaborate pulpit. There may well be a much greater similarity in the homes of these believers. The issue is seen sometimes to revolve around the nature of corporate worship. And even in this case there is still the question of what constitutes beauty – simplicity of line and form has always had a great attraction.

Whatever the tradition or theology the human spirit longs to shape, make or create things of beauty in one way or another. If not paintings, then music; if not music, then preaching and so on. It is as if the stones themselves would cry out if this spirit were completely suppressed! My own background is in words and literature rather than pictures, and so I am acutely aware of the need to let the pictures speak for themselves. Some of these works of art have spoken so profoundly to me that my own personal pilgrimage of faith has been both challenged and enriched.

It is no surprise that pictorial images have had such a significant effect on the development of the Christian faith. Without a biblical background that the artists take for granted they cannot speak as effectively as they might, but words without such images can be very blunt and inappropriate instruments. It is in the hope that a proper interplay between words and images is possible that this book is offered to you. May you too find yourself kneeling in wonder at the beauty, awe and mystery at the heart of all things, however ordinary, and revealed especially and uniquely in Jesus Christ.

Keith J. White

MASTERPIECES
OF THE
BIBLE

OLD
TESTAMENT

'The Ancient of Days'

William Blake

(1757–1827)
Before 1795, 235 x 170 cm.
British Museum, London

Artistic Background

Blake was a poet, an illustrator, an engraver and a Christian mystic almost totally at odds with the artistic and philosophical world of his time. His understanding of the nature of God and His relationship with creation was as unorthodox as his art. His whole life was focused on his personal perception and visions. He was concerned not with outward appearances (realism) but with what he saw with his 'inner eye.' There is evidence of his sympathy for Michelangelo and Raphael, also of a deep knowledge of the Bible and the writings of Milton, Shakespeare and Dante. His work is timeless and symbolic, equally accessible to each successive generation because of its delicate balance between symbolism and spiritual content. The picture is a metalcut with watercolour.

"I was there when he set the heavens in place, when he marked out the horizon on the face of the deep."

Biblical Background

(Proverbs 8:22-27 and Daniel 7:9-14)
The term 'Ancient of Days' is used to describe God in one of Daniel's dreams. The description reads: "His clothing was as white as snow; the hair of his head was white like wool. His throne was flaming with fire, and its wheels were all ablaze. A river of fire was flowing, coming out from before him." Blake applied aspects of this to the passage in Proverbs where Wisdom recounts the creation of the material universe: "he set the heavens in place – he set a compass on the face of the depths ..."

Reflecting on the Painting

Although Blake is actually portraying an earlier part of God's creation, the echoes of Michelangelo's God in the creation of Adam (page 14) are not hard to see. God crouches over an abyss, his hair blown horizontally by a primal wind. His glory is represented by the red orb which surrounds him and creates a golden light. This light pierces both the surrounding very dark and ominous clouds, and also the edge of the abyss.

In his left hand God divides the light from the darkness by using a pair of compasses. They are realistic yet meant to be supernatural. The fact that Blake intends them to be seen as symbolic is underlined by their resemblance to flashes of lightning in the darkness. His overall purpose is not to aid understanding of how God looks or how he created the universe, but to represent the elemental conflict between good and evil, order and chaos, and the fundamental tension between the spiritual and the physical.

Many Christians have found Blake's faith and theology disturbing yet the profundity of his vision and his understanding of the Bible encourage others to see through, not with, the eye, and so discover new realms and dimensions of reality.

We may be struck by the sheer daring of his imagination as he explores a moment of creation almost impossible to imagine, let alone portray. Do we have our own alternative?

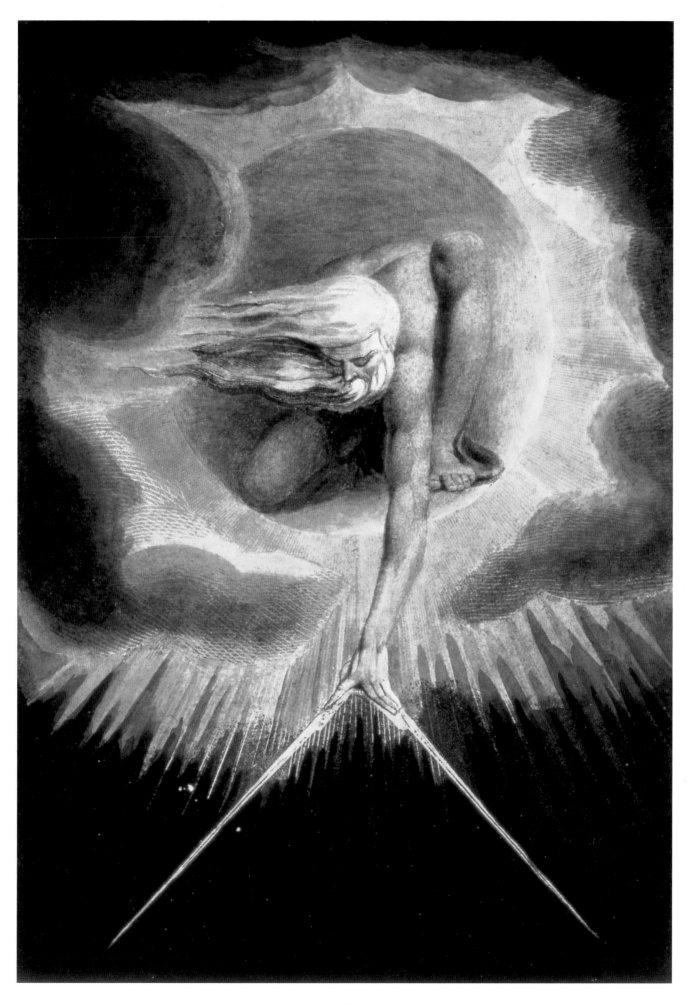

The Creation of Adam

Michelangelo (Buonarroti)
(1475–1564)
1508–12, Larger than lifesize
Sistine Chapel, Rome

Artistic Background

This fresco, which is part of one of the greatest works of art ever produced, the ceiling of the Sistine Chapel in Rome, took four years to complete. The theme is the story of the world before the coming of Christ. The centre, of which this section is a part, illustrates the origin of the world, humanity, and sin. This is surrounded by prophets and sibyls who announce Christ's coming, who are in turn surrounded by Christ's forefathers. Michelangelo's mastery of the ideal human form is a vital element in this picture, but he has succeeded in communicating the spiritual and divine through, not despite, his minute attention to personal and anatomical detail. (See also page 76.)

"So God created man in his own image, in the image of God he created him; male and female he created them."

Biblical Background

(Genesis 1:1–2:8)

The origin of all things as recounted in the first book of the Bible is an epic of six days. God speaks and light, sky, earth, plants, stars, living creatures appear at his command. His final act is the creation of mankind. The words used in Genesis 2:7 are: "the Lord God formed the man from the dust of the ground and breathed into his nostrils the breath of life and the man became a living being."

Reflecting on the Painting

This one part of the vast Sistine painting symbolises the mystery of the whole of creation. God the Father, full of power, purpose and wisdom, supported by an entourage of angels, moves effortlessly and majestically through space and time. He personifies creative energy. His movement, company and sense of powerful intensity contrast with the languid loneliness of Adam. Adam is still almost one with the earth from which he has been moulded. He is alive yet he seems to be awaking from a primal sleep, gazing longingly into the eyes of his Creator. But Michelangelo intends us to focus further in on the index fingers of God and Adam and that minute space between them charged with potential energy. God's finger represents his nature and purpose; Adam's is slowly reaching out. The breath of life is about to flow into Adam. The moment of literal creation is about to take place; history is about to begin, for what we call history is the product, and also the nature, of that famous gap between the fingers. Michelangelo will trace great themes of this history on the Sistine Ceiling. But the detail, though concentrating on a split second of time, represents an eternal truth: God is always seeking to bring spiritual life to His creation. Time and eternity, the physical and the spiritual, are always interacting as a result of His initiative. The Incarnation, when the Word became flesh, is a revisiting of that gap which manifests itself in one way or another until the end of time.

Expulsion from Paradise

Masaccio (Tommaso di Giovanni)
(1401–28)
c.1425–28. Detail
Brancacci Chapel of Santa Maria del Carmine, Florence

Artistic Background

Masaccio lived less than 30 years but his works – altar-pieces, panels and frescoes, reveal an original approach to his familiar subject-matter. He was influenced by Giotto in that he sought to portray human emotion through the figures rather than through symbolic or allegorical references. At a time when much painting was highly decorative and formal, his is very tight and austere. He helped to forge a way for those who were to study nature and the human form and paint it with sympathetic realism. This detail is part of a larger fresco.

Biblical Background
(Genesis 2:4–3:24)

Adam and Eve were created to enjoy paradise. They were to take responsibility for the garden of Eden. The one restrictive command they were given by God was not to eat from the tree of the knowledge of good and evil. Tempted by the serpent Eve ate this fruit and shared it with her husband. They immediately realised their nakedness and hid from God. He told them the dire consequences of their disobedience, drove them from the garden and prevented them from returning to the tree of life with cherubim and a flaming sword.

Reflecting on the Painting

The drama and meaning of the event Masaccio portrays is all too clear. The two dejected and anguished figures of Adam and Eve are driven by an angel with a powerful sword from the gate of paradise. The angel is painted traditionally, with wings; God's voice is represented by the lines emanating from the gate.

But the undeniable focus of Masaccio's painting are Adam and Eve. They are punished in a way that emphasises their solidarity and shared predicament – their forms make a soft and harmonious whole. Their flesh is painted with a realism made more striking by the obviously conventional fig leaves which are almost certainly a censor's afterthought! Though the figures are not painted with Michaelangelo's or Leonardo's precision, the intention is to depict real people and real emotion. They have a great dignity and even in this moment of judgement they are still a wonderful creation.

These are not images or personifactions of shame, guilt, repentance; they are real people who feel and express the horror, the sense of unbearable loss their actions have caused. But as we enter into their feelings they can embody for us universal loss and suffering in human form. Yet above them the angel seems almost to shelter them, the curve of his body linking to the curve of Adam's back. It is the reverse of so many pictures which show an alienated seraph fiercely barring the gates of Paradise. Masaccio thus depicts the intensity of their emotion without relief or seeming comfort because he knew this event was part of a greater narrative. It was in perfect human form that salvation would come – in the flesh of Jesus Christ.

> *"So the Lord God banished him from the Garden of Eden to work the ground from which he had been taken."*

The Exile from the Ark and the Drunkenness of Noah

Anonymous (known as 'Master of the Munich Golden Legend')
1423, 20.7 x 14 cm.
British Library, London

Artistic Background

This full-page illustration is one of four Old Testament scenes in what is known as *The Bedford Book of Hours*. The book was a wedding present to the Duke of Bedford and Anne of Burgundy and there are personalised mottoes and coats of arms at seven different places in it. The idea behind such a treasured personal present was that devout lay Christians could have their own prayer and devotional study guide. Books of Hours followed closely the worship patterns of monasteries and religious orders and took their names from the daily services. Another depiction of the three scenes: the Flood, the sacrifice and the drunkenness of Noah is found in the Sistine Chapel, by Michelangelo.

Biblical Background
(Genesis 8:15–9:23)

After the flood subsided, the ark built by Noah came to rest on dry ground. The animals and birds were let out to find fresh pastures and lands. Noah offered a sacrifice as a sign of his thankfulness to God, and then he and his family set about recultivating the earth and building homes and shelter. Embarrassingly, and as a reminder of the frailty of even those God uses for special purposes, Noah got drunk from the vine produced at his vineyard and one of his sons had to cover his nakedness.

Reflecting on the Picture

It's probably a good thing that the artist has chosen a moment when the ark is on firm ground because, sturdy though it is, it doesn't look seaworthy! It has previously served its purpose well for all the animals and birds are in superb condition as they fly, strut, graze or explore their new environment. They form a contrast to the rather cold, rough sea which recedes to reveal bones, carcasses and the remains of castles and towns. The sea is as full of the remains of death as the earth is full of the variety and promise of life. The details of life and death range from the olive branch in the beak of the dove to the carrion crow eating the carcass of one of those who perished.

Meanwhile as Mrs. Noah carefully helps the remaining animals across the gangplank-cum-draw-bridge watched by one of her daughters-in-law, three stages in the life of Noah are shown. First he kneels at a burnt offering; then he supervises the cultivation of a vineyard. Finally he falls back drunk from the wine so recently grown and trodden in the wooden vat by one of his sons. Another son hurries to cover his nakedness.

All of this takes place at the express command or under the eye of God. His face is cloaked but His glory is clearly portrayed.

It could hardly be a better subject for a book of hours. The detail means the reader will never tire of exploring the picture, while the combination of sacred and secular, of life and death, faithfulness and drunkenness, is an exact and careful setting for the story of Jesus and the redemption of mankind, as well as a reminder of the stuff of everyday life. If you ever have a chance to look at the book itself the relationship of this picture to the one before (the building of the ark) and the one after (the tower of Babel) is beautifully handled. Though remote in time because of its subject matter and conventions, it is a world we know all too well from personal experience.

"Never again will all life be cut off by the waters of a flood; never again will there be a flood to destroy the earth."

Comēt noel aps le deluge arnua a teire et muist lprs le bestail et fist sacrifice et planta la vigne

Tower of Babel

Maurits Escher

(1898–1972)
1928, Woodcut 62.2 x 38.6 cm.
Gemeente Museum, The Hague

Artistic Background

The work of Escher is so unusual that some dispute whether it should be called 'art' at all. (He is not mentioned in the *Thames and Hudson Dictionary of Art and Artists*, 1994 edition, for example.) Escher's chosen media were woodcuts and lithographs. He approached the visible world with a sense of amazement and awe, aware of the great enigmas and paradoxes of time, space, infinity and eternity. He has wrestled with the core issues of modern mathematics and physics, as did the Cubists, Dadaists and Surrealists, but he did so in a way immediately attractive and comprehensive to lay people because of his insistence on visual and rational coherence.

Biblical Background

(Genesis 11:1-9)

The story of the building of the city of Babel (Babylon) and its tower is, like that of Noah's ark, of great significance in Jewish and Christian theology. The whole enterprise was characterised by human pride – whether in its scale or technology. God's will and purpose are not even considered by the builders! He intervenes to stop the building and to sow confusion among human beings. From this point on the world is full of tribes, nations and many different languages. Some have seen Pentecost (Acts 2) as a divine reversal of this event, where the potential for understanding and fellowship is made possible by the Holy Spirit.

"Come, let us build ourselves a city, with a tower that reaches to the heavens, so that we may make a name for ourselves...."

Reflecting on the Woodcut

Those familiar with Escher will instantly recognise this as his work because of the dramatic and unusual perspective and from the neat, almost mathematical, precision. It is similar to an architect's drawing. We are given something of God's view of events as envisaged by the story. A thriving, well-ordered city and seaport is dominated by a tower of indeterminate style (Egyptian? Byzantine?) which dwarfs all else.

At a certain point in studying the work it dawns on us that Escher has chosen a momentous moment in the story: what seems like a purposeful scene full of activity is, in fact, the exact time when all meaningful work and communication has ended. If you trace all possible ropes, pulleys and lines of communication, you find they lead nowhere. The project has ceased. Technically it all seems feasible (there is still adequate rope and material) but it has grown too big. The limits of human endeavour have been reached.

At the top the obvious breakdown in communication between workers is portrayed. Pride awaits its fall.

On the highest bricks reaching out to the heavens sits a worker. Is he asking for help? Is he blaming God for the failure? Has he realised the futility of the building of any city without the Lord's help? Escher gives no clue, but his archetypal work still serves as a timeless commentary upon continuing proud human enterprise ranging from cities to empires, scientific experiments to 'final solutions.'

Lot Fleeing with His Daughters from Sodom

Albrecht Dürer
(1471–1528)
c.1498, 52 x 41 cm.
National Gallery, Washington DC

Artistic Background

Like other artists of genius Dürer was able to work in any number of materials and to address a huge range of subjects. His work is full of surprises deriving from his originality of technique and conception. This panel treats a dramatic subject in an unusual way. His technique using oil and tempera is assured in the balance of colour, in composition, in the accurate and loving representation of the flora, and the portraitist's attention to details in the three figures. There are no obvious precursors or comparative works.

Biblical Background
(Genesis 18:20–19:38)

The wickedness of the Dead Sea cities of Sodom and Gomorrah was so great that even Abraham's pleas for mercy did not save them. Following a narrow escape from gang rape Lot and his family were warned by divine messengers to flee. His sons-in-law thought he was joking; his wife looked back and was turned into a pillar of salt; only Lot and his two daughters escaped the destruction of the cities by fire and brimstone. They travelled via the small city of Zoar for a cave, where the daughters were to commit incest with their drunken father.

Reflecting on the Picture

The three figures seem quite incongruous, so prim and proper, set against a scene of almost cosmic devastation and destruction. The glow of the fire infuses the whole picture. They are far from typical refugees – the daughters' hair is meticulously done and Lot, dressed in his fine turban, has chosen to carry a flask of wine and a basket of eggs.

The vegetation around them serves to highlight the contrast between their new life and the barrenness of the world they have left. Lot's wife remains, a small, still figure fixed forever like a rock in the landscape.

Typical of Dürer, however, is an underlying subtlety and exploration of the story. One of the sins in Sodom specifically referred to is that of sexual immorality. Yet the two daughters, in order to ensure the continuation of their family line, are about to commit incest with their father. Another symbolism becomes clear – the parted sheepskin smock of Lot, the partly lifted skirt of the daughter in red, and the glance and keys of the other daughter.

We find such an ambivalence about the whole proceedings it is difficult to know how to react. Dürer has been able to transcend time and convention in recreating a famous and influential image which combines death, idolatry, sexuality, refugees and family loyalty in a way that speaks afresh centuries later.

> *"Hurry and get out of this place, because the LORD is about to destroy the city."*

23

Rebecca at the Well

Giovanni Antonio Pellegrini
(1675–41). Detail
c.1708–1713, 127.3 x 104.5 cm.
National Gallery, London

Artistic Background

Pellegrini was a Venetian painter who travelled widely in Europe, enhancing the reputation of Venice in Germany, France, the Low Countries and England, where he stayed for several years. While in England he helped in the painting of scenery for a production at the Haymarket theatre. He worked on a range of biblical, historical and classical themes using fast thick fluent brushstrokes. Studying under Ricci and Pagani, he in turn was influential in British art, especially at Castle Howard. The painting is done on canvas.

Biblical Background
(Genesis 24)

When Abraham's wife, Sara died, he asked his servant, Eliezer, to find a wife for Isaac, his only son by her. Eliezer was to go back to Mesopotamia, Abraham's original land, rather than choose someone from among the Canaanites. Coming to a well he waited for a woman who would offer both him and his camels water to drink. This would be the Lord's sign that the woman was the wife intended for Isaac. When Rebecca did just this he gave her a bracelet and other jewellery. Her family listened to Eliezer's story and agreed to the marriage.

Reflecting on the Painting

One of the striking things about this picture is the way in which Rebecca seems to have been transferred straight from eighteenth century England back in time. Her dress, her skin, her hair and face, as well as the water jug and the head of the lion spurting water, reveal her origins. Given the choice of surrounding colours it is obvious that Pellegrini intended her dress, cloak, blouse and appearance to stand out dramatically. It is sunset but the white of her skin seems unaffected. The camels look inscrutable, and their driver, holding a stick, turns away. Eliezer gazes intently at Rebecca, his strong arm, bald head, rugged beard and dark skin contrasting in every way with her.

He has given her the bracelet and she now wears it (but not the nose-ring which would have been rather out of place in the eighteenth century!). She seems to be indicating where her family lives and inviting Eliezer to meet them.

So why this quite extraordinary contrast and conscious anachronism?

"As for me, the Lord has led me on the journey to the house of my master's relatives"

Contrasting beautiful young women with aged, rough men was a popular Baroque subject. But is there something more? Does the encounter make reference to other biblical narratives? Some have linked it with the meeting between Jesus and the woman at the well in Samaria (John 4). There may also be an allusion to God's chosen one. If so, the jewels and camels anticipate the adoration of the wise men; Eliezer's rustic appearance brings echoes of the shepherds and the servant, a harbinger, John the Baptist. It is possible, but whatever the truth the gaze between the two is intended to arrest our attention and leave room for our imagination to work.

Jacob with the Flock of Laban

Jusepe de Ribera
(c.1590–1652)
1638, 132 x 118 cm.
National Gallery, London

Artistic Background

Though born in Spain, Ribera spent most of his working life in Naples. His love for realism (painting from observation) rather than mannerism (painting in accordance with or reaction to traditions) echoes the naturalistic style of Caravaggio. It is also typical of a Spanish down-to-earth approach to life. His best known paintings are of cruelty and terror, so this picture reveals an unexpected tenderness. It is a fragment of a larger canvas.

Biblical Background
(Genesis 30:25-43)

Having fled from his brother Esau, whom he tricked into giving away his birthright, Jacob was himself outwitted by his uncle Laban into working for him for fourteen years. As wages Jacob asked only for the speckled sheep in his uncle's flocks. Laban hid all these but Jacob found a way of producing a great deal more. After 6 years he left with this self-bred flock.

Reflecting on the Picture

In this reduced painting (the original stretched to the left and would have portrayed more sheep drinking) we see what is in effect a portrait of Jacob. His right hand lightly strokes one of his flock, his left hand grips his shepherd's staff, while he looks up towards Heaven. After years of waiting, and serving an exploitive uncle, he still trusts the promise of God in his vision at Bethel where he was told he would be the father of a great nation living in the land around Bethel (Genesis 28:10-22).

His sense of peace and acceptance of the divine will is emphasized by the harmony of the picture as a whole; he is at one with nature in both colour and form. His dress blends with the autumn shades, and his body seems almost part of the tree against which he is resting.

With no further mechanisms or devices we find a scene pregnant with meaning and allusion. Jacob is a good shepherd – archetype of the good shepherd so beloved by the psalmists and the prophets, forerunner to Jesus himself who sacrificed not 14 years, but life itself. The tree brings thoughts of both the tree of life and the cross/tree on which Jesus gave his life.

"I am with you and will watch over you wherever you go."

And the lamb represents the Lamb of God. Tantalisingly, we cannot see whether it is speckled or without blemish due to Ribera's use of light and shade. While the focus of Jacob and the rest of the flock is elsewhere his lamb looks intently at us, transcending time, place and story, precursor of the Lamb of God that takes away the sin of the world.

Joseph in Egypt

Jacopo da Pontormo

(1494–1556/7)
c.1515, 44 x 49 cm.
National Gallery, London

Artistic Background

Portormo is best known for his frescoes in a Medici villa, and 'The Deposition of Christ.' He is termed a 'Mannerist,' in that he valued the way in which Leonardo, Michangelo and Raphael painted an ideal of beauty, and strove for novelties and insights beyond Nature itself. This painting was one of fourteen panels intended for a nuptial chamber. Among his innovations was the simultaneous presentation of a whole story on one panel. There is also a mixture of realism and fantasy, contemporary and historical material.

Biblical Background
(Genesis 37–50)

Joseph was the favourite of Jacob's twelve sons, who were to give their name to the tribes of Israel. The others became jealous of him and he was sold by them into slavery in Egypt. Despite setbacks his intelligence and honesty were eventually rewarded with a senior position in Egypt. When famine hit his family in Canaan they turned to Egypt for food, where they were reunited with their brother Joseph. They settled and it was here that the descendants of Jacob became numerous. Joseph's story has often been seen as a prefiguring of that of Christ in several respects.

Reflecting on the Painting

The picture is best considered as what we would now call a strip cartoon. It records at least four successive scenes from the story of the life of Joseph. They begin in the bottom left-hand corner and end at the top right-hand corner. The whole is something like a stage set with steps, a cylindrical building and staircase. This makes possible such a sequence without any sense of confusion. Portormo has little interest in recreating an authentic Egyptian architectural style, but intense interest in the characters who are part of the narrative.

"Do not be distressed and do not be angry with yourselves for selling me here, because it was to save lives that God sent me ahead of you."

In scene one, Joseph introduces his brothers to the Pharoah of Egypt. The three pictured are in postures showing their extreme gratitude and deference. The blue tunic of the kneeling brother stands out in the whole picture and emphasises his obeisance.

In scene two we see Joseph being pulled in a carriage while a crowd is so keen to praise him it has to be restrained. Joseph is listening attentively to the plea of a citizen kneeling and showing him a document.

In scene three Joseph leads one of his two sons, Ephraim and Manasseh, up the spiral staircase while his mother, Rachel, greets the other child warmly.

The final scene is Jacob's deathbed. Ephraim and Manasseh join others around the bed of the dying Jacob as he gives them his blessing. The erring brothers are passive figures throughout; Joseph, in contrast, is a dynamic and sympathetic character.

Watching everything is a crowd whose motives are unclear. Each member of the group is painted with great care and individuality. Set amidst bright and contrasting colours, statues, a kaleidoscope of characters and geometrical shapes, they complete a picture of surprising unity and depth.

The Brazen Serpent

Giambattista Tiepolo
(1696–1770)
c.1731–32, 167 x 311 cm.
Venice, Gallerie dell'Accademia

Artistic Background

A Venetian who eventually moved to Madrid, Tiepolo was probably the outstanding Italian painter of the 18th century. He produced works for churches, religious orders and secular patrons throughout Europe. His style and range is varied but his larger pieces, including frescoes, are characterised by bold decoration, outstanding blues, and a sense of brightness and lightness. This is a detail of a large canvas which was badly damaged as a result of having been rolled. It was designed as one of thirteen biblical stories for a church serving a community of Benedictine nuns, and to be placed above the eye level of the worshippers.

"Make a snake and put it up on a pole. Anyone who is bitten can look at it and live."

Biblical Background

(Numbers 21:6-9; John 3:14-15)
One of the trials the Israelites faced on their long and tortuous journey from Egypt, across the Red Sea, through the desert to the Promised Land was an attack by poisonous snakes. As many were dying the people pleaded with Moses to help: "We have sinned. Pray that the Lord will take the snakes away from us." The Lord's answer was that Moses should make a bronze snake and put in on a pole. Anyone who looked at it would live. When, many centuries later, Jesus was talking to a Pharisee called Nicodemus, he used this story of the bronze serpent to illustrate the manner and meaning of his own death.

Reflecting on the Picture

Moses has erected the serpent on a rough branch of a tree. In his right hand he holds the rod of office; his left points to the serpent. Like a prophet he is calling to the people to repent and look to their only hope of salvation. Meanwhile the death and suffering caused by the snakes is powerfully illustrated by the figures in the foreground. One figure on the right is desperately struggling with snakes. He looks doomed despite his obvious strength, for he is not looking at the bronze serpent, the source of healing. The rest of the figures represent many different varieties of suffering, need, relationship and attitude. A child is brought to the serpent; another person prays. Together they represent the needs and sins of the world. It is Tiepolo's intention that they should be studied carefully.

Tiepolo, like so many of the artists who painted Old Testament subjects, sees in them a metaphor or prefiguring of the life of Christ and the church. The images are especially potent. The serpents remind us of the origin of sin in the Garden of Eden; their deadly bites represent the power of sin which leads to death; the struggles and pleading of the people demonstrate the human predicament; Moses represents the word of God and the pole bearing the serpent was, as Jesus intimated himself, a symbol of his sacrifical death on the cross. Salvation is only possible by looking to this sacrifice in faith. "As Moses lifted up the serpent in the wilderness even so the Son of Man must be lifted up, that everyone who believes in him may have eternal life."

The Scapegoat

Holman Hunt
(1827–1910)
1856, 87 x 139 cm.
Lady Lever Art Gallery, Port Sunlight, England

Artistic Background

The pre-Raphaelites, of whom Hunt was one, were a group of British Victorian artists seeking to return art to a state of 'purity' by choosing significant subjects and a simplicity of colour, style and accuracy in relation to nature. So determined was Hunt to get the details of this picture right that he began it beside the Dead Sea and used four goats during the course of its execution. The colours of the painting are so bright that they have been described as lurid. One of his fellow pre-Raphaelites, Ford Madox Brown, called it "one of the most tragic and impressive works in the annals of art!" Others rate it as a poor artistic work. It certainly disturbs for whatever reason.

Biblical Background

(Leviticus 16:5-22; Isaiah 1:18; 53:4) On the Jewish Day of Atonement one of two goats was chosen to be a scapegoat. The High Priest laid his hands on the head of the goat and confessed the sins of the Israelites. The sins were thus symbolically transferred onto the goat which was then taken and released into the desert. Hunt has linked this symbolically with the prophecy of Isaiah, which tells of sins which are scarlet becoming white as snow, and the suffering servant 'carrying the sorrows' of mankind.

"He shall send the goat away into the desert ... The goat will carry on itself all their sins to a solitary place."

Reflecting on the Painting

Because this is one of two paintings of the same subject by Hunt, a knowledge of the other version helps to confirm his intention and symbolism.

The solitary goat is set against a barren landscape at sunset. Its feet are sinking through the salt-encrusted surface of the desert. It is a scene of unrelieved desolation whether one looks at the skeletons, the shrivelled plants, or the bare mountains. The goat seems to be staggering either from exhaustion and thirst, or as if under an unbearable weight.

Its horns are wrapped with scarlet wool, a symbol of the sins of the nation, echoing Isaiah's description. The sheer isolation of the goat recalls the desolation of Christ, the sinbearer, when he cried, "My God, my God, why hast thou forsaken me?"

The colours of the painting cry out for attention. Are they really drawn from observation? It is here that the other version helps us to understand their significance. In that picture there is a rainbow; the scapegoat is superimposed on the narrative of the Flood. This is a direct reference to God's covenant that He will not destroy the earth by flood again. In this vision the rainbow is symbolised by the colours themselves. Although the sunset is no comfort to the goat its light symbolises to us God's covenant love. Sin and death do not have the final word in God's world, however savage their effects may be.

The Visit of the Queen of Sheba to King Solomon

Edward John Poynter
(1836–1919)
1884–90, 253.5 x 350.5 cm.
The Art Gallery of New South Wales, Sydney

Artistic Background

Poynter was a leading figure in English Victorian art circles and became director of the National Gallery and president of the Royal Academy. He concentrated on reconstructions of Greek, Roman and Egyptian civilisations in medieval legends and biblical stories. He shows the Victorian tendency to elaborate on any theme, and gave minute attention to detail. This huge work is his most ambitious and was based on careful research and painstaking drawings of every component. He had worked on illustrations for a Bible and was thoroughly conversant with both the details and the setting of his subjects.

"I did not believe ... until I came and saw with my own eyes."

Biblical Background
(2 Chronicles 8:1–9:28)

David's son, Solomon, was renowned for his wisdom, wealth and power. He built the great temple in Jerusalem and erected a magnificent palace for himself using slave labour to complete his bold schemes. His palace is not described in the sort of detail devoted to the temple (eg. 2 Chronicles 2:1–6:11) but Poynter takes his cue from the record of his throne (2 Chronicles 9:17-19) and palace furnishings to assume that the palace was of equal magnificence. The Queen of Sheba has heard of Solomon's greatness but even she is bowled over by the scale of his achievements: "The half had never been told." Not surprisingly all this was done at the expense of the poorer citizens of the kingdom of Solomon and the future unity of the Jewish nation.

Reflecting on the Painting

The purpose of the picture is to recreate a biblical scene of unique grandeur with as much accuracy as possible. The pillars of the temple create a sense of vastness and space. The throne is represented as described in the biblical text with a lion on each of its six steps.

The assembled throng focuses without exception on the momentous encounter between queen and king. The Queen of Sheba mounts the steps indicating the array of gifts she has brought. Solomon strides down from his throne to greet her, his right hand seeming to indicate either his blessing or his wish that she should not concern herself with gifts. The scene has been arranged in every aspect to heighten the dramatic moment of their historic meeting.

Some have seen the queen's visit symbolising the Gentile world coming to honour the Law, just as the Magi represented this world coming to worship Christ.

It may be that this was the sum total of Poynter's intent. But there is the underlying theological question to be asked: is Solomon a representative of the glory of Yahweh or has he taken to himself much of the honour due to his creator God? The history of kingship in Israel is ambivalent from start to finish because properly speaking God is Israel's only king. The queen concludes her visit with an observation on this very theme and we are left with a sense of uncertainty as we reflect on the meaning of the picture: is this the kingdom and kingship appropriate to the chosen people of the Lord?

Vision of Ezekiel

Raphael (Raffaello Sanzio)

(1483–1520)
c.1518, 40 x 30 cm.
Uffizi, Florence

Artistic Background

As a Renaissance artist Raphael sought to combine Greek and Roman traditions with those of the Bible. His understanding of Yahweh was therefore influenced by the Roman god Jupiter. This highlights the problem any artist has in trying to portray God – every attempt is bound to be biased and partial, reflecting the conventions and assumptions of a particular time and place. We may feel that these sometimes come between us and God rather than enhancing our understanding. What Raphael does here is to use every resource at his command to reinforce the sense of glory of the divine majesty. The medium used is oil on a panel.

Biblical Background

(Ezekiel 1:1-14; also Ezekiel 10:14 and Revelation 4:6-8)

Ezekiel was one of the Jewish people taken captive and living as exiles in Babylon. There he had a series of visions in which the heavens were opened, and which form the basis of much subsequent understanding of the divine nature (including the book of Revelation). In this first vision an immense cloud in a windstorm was surrounded with brilliant light. The centre was like a fire. There were four living creatures – an ox, a lion, an eagle and a man. The man, who represented the glory of the Lord, spoke to Ezekiel, calling him to a mission to his people. The power of the vision was such that Ezekiel never deviated from this calling.

"In the thirtieth year, in the fourth month on the fifth day ... the heavens were opened and I saw visions of God."

Reflecting on the Painting

Raphael has been careful both to study the biblical narrative in his picture, and to adapt it in such a way that enhances the coherence and unity of his work. God moves above the firmament supported by playful cherubim and the four creatures (the 'tetramorph' later identified as the four evangelists). The six creatures, or beings, together with the central figure (who represents God) form an almost perfect whole, solid yet moving and with spaces in the togetherness. The colours representing the story of God are accentuated by the sombre surrounding clouds and silhouetted wings, while the spaces between the interwoven figures provide the opportunity for that glory to shine through. The realism of the figures and their skin colours means that the whole is dominated by the yellow and gold of divinity.

The eyes of the divine representation in this vision focus on the diminutive figure of Ezekiel at the bottom left-hand corner of the picture. The contrasts of scale could hardly be greater without Ezekiel disappearing completely! The shaft of light in which he is caught is part of a landscape which is separate from the vision. It is as if there are two realities, a heavenly and earthly, linked only by that shaft. In this way Raphael underlines his awareness that it is a vision, not an historical event: real and overwhelming to us and to Ezekiel, but one to which many of Ezekiel's hearers are blind.

It is possible that Raphael's depiction of this vision has done as much as the written word for many to convey the essence of the divine glory.

The Three Men in the Fiery Furnace

Wall painting from the Priscilla Catacomb, Rome
3rd century approx.

Artistic Background

In the years following the spread of Christianity throughout the Roman Empire there was so much persecution that the followers of the Way became an underground church. They buried their dead in catacombs, called 'cemeteries' or sleeping places, which later became the meeting places for the celebration of communion and preaching, as well as hiding places. It was in these hundreds of miles of underground passages that some of the first recorded Christian art is to be found. The purpose of these very simple scenes was to instruct and inspire at a critical time in the life of the Faith. They concentrate on famous Bible stories and hold out a promise of salvation and hope. Death is not the end: the true destiny of the human race is beyond the present world.

"They saw that the fire had not harmed their bodies, nor was a hair of their heads singed; their robes were not scorched, and there was no smell of fire on them."

Biblical Background
(Daniel 3)

When King Nebuchadnezzar of Babylon erected a huge statue and ordered everyone to worship it, three Jewish officials refused to do so, mindful of the commandments (Exodus 20). They were thrown into a furnace as a punishment. As the King watched them thrown into the flames he was astonished to see them joined by a fourth figure. He called them out, recognising the intervention of God, and ordered that this God should be respected. He believed the fourth figure to be an angel.

Reflecting on the Painting

The painting is so simple it is almost childlike, and consists of very few brush strokes. The three figures are in almost identical Persian dress; the flames couldn't be more economically indicated. The only other symbol is that of a dove.

But pausing before the picture and recreating the darkness of the cave in which it was found, it's message becomes not only clear, but powerful. The early Christians who saw it knew only too well the dilemma of Shadrach, Meshach and Abednego, for they were threatened with a similar punishment if they didn't acknowledge the Roman Emperor as divine. The three figures look directly at us, their hands raised in the typical praying ('orans') position of early Christian art and the flames are ineffective, almost incidental. The dove symbolises God's help and presence. He has come alongside them in their tribulation. There is a solidarity in the fellowship of the three with their hands interposed, which the Holy Spirit makes possible or reinforces. It may not be that the early beholders would escape death, but they knew that in and through God's presence and help they would know eternal fellowship and communion through it.

Like so many events depicted by early Christians this was seen as a type of resurrection. They recast Old Testament stories in the light of the resurrection of Christ, which was their single cause for hope amidst persecution and oppression.

Belshazzar's Feast

Rembrandt Van Rijn
(1606–69)
1635,168 x 209 cm.
National Gallery, London

Artistic Background

Whereas Catholic artists of Rembrandt's time could paint for church buildings (altar screens and frescoes in particular), the Protestant/Calvinist churches were intentionally bare. This meant he painted biblical scenes for private homes. This dramatic scene gives Rembrandt the opportunity to display many of his skills: a superb technique, a sense of structural balance, the use of contrasts between light and dark and portraiture. The Hebrew letters are accurately written from top to bottom, and this incorporates a suggestion of a Jewish friend and neighbour, that this was why the writing could not be understood by anyone except Daniel. The medium is oil on canvas.

"Suddenly the fingers of a human hand appeared and wrote on the plaster of the wall ... The king watched the hand as it wrote."

Biblical Background
(Daniel 5)

The King of Babylon, Belshazzar, gave a feast for a thousand nobles. As the wine flowed he ordered the sacred vessels stolen from the temple at Jerusalem by his father, Nebuchadnezzar, to be brought in. It was an act of sacrilege compounded when they toasted gods of gold, silver, bronze, iron, wood and stone. Suddenly a human hand appeared and shocked the assembly as it wrote on the plaster of the palace wall. No one in the court could decipher the message and so Daniel, an exile from Judah, was summoned. He alone interpreted the sombre message, and that very night King Belshazzar was slain.

Reflecting on the Painting

The splendour and grandeur of the feast is represented not by numbers of guests but by the extraordinary finery of the king's robes, the jewellery and robes of his closest guests, and the gold and silver vessels. It is the vessels that symbolise the extreme act of idolatry which challenges the God of the Hebrews. The king is the central figure in the picture and he dominates the scene. He and his guests are horrified, and their inward fear is captured not only in their faces, but in the turmoil and disequilibrium of the scene. A dish is overturned and two goblets spill their wine. The contrast between this finery and richly textured clothing and the simplicity of the hand and the message could hardly be greater. The message: "Mene, Mene, Tekel, Upharsin," is God's judgement on Belshazzar and his rule. Their riches cannot protect them and sheer fear shows on all their faces.

As the viewer's eye roves from face to hand, to finery, to the divine message and back, a final, mysterious figure is revealed. To the left of the scene a piper continues to play. Whatever he started is now almost certainly a dirge. The presence of a similar figure occurs also in 'Return of the Prodigal Son.' Once again it is possible that this is Rembrandt. Like Bach's great biblical music this judgement demands a personal response. The viewer can no more escape this than Belshazzar can escape his fate.

MASTERPIECES
OF THE
BIBLE

NEW
TESTAMENT

The Madonna del Granduca

Raphael (Raffaelo Sanzio)
(1483-1520)
c.1505, 81 x 53.6 cm.
Palazzo Pitti, Florence

Artistic Background

When Raphael arrived in Florence two of the world's greatest artists, Michelangelo and Leonardo da Vinci, were at the height of their powers. He was inspired, not overawed. He understood perhaps better than anyone before him the notion of balance and dynamics of form in a painting. Though he painted some magnificent altarpieces and frescoes, one of his most enduring influences has probably been in the pictures of Mary. He enhanced a rich tradition of representations of Madonna and Child. This one is known technically as a 'Theotokos Eleousa' and stresses the tender and affectionate relationship. The medium is oil.

Biblical Background

(Matthew 1:18-25; 2:1-12; Luke 2:1-7) The relationship between Mary and Jesus is one of the most special and pivotal in the Christian story. Whereas the relationship between a mother and son is always close, that between Jesus and his mother is unique in that there was no human father. Mary was chosen as a highly favoured virgin to give birth to the Son of God, the Saviour of the world. During his life she was often with him and followed him to his death and the tomb.

"The virgin will be with child and will give birth to a son, and they will call him Immanuel—which means 'God with us.'"

Reflecting on the Painting

The painting seems familiar even if we haven't previously encountered it, because of the many others on this theme before and after that have used a similar composition. There is a perfect sense of completeness and peace about the characters and also the composition of this painting. This comes from a complex and almost indefinable combination of colours, forms, dynamics, technique and yet classical simplicity.

Mary, her pure face gently inclined, has a look that conveys her servanthood as a vehicle for God's will, but also a sense of wonder as she ponders the meaning of the birth of the Saviour of the World. Is there, too, a hint of sadness as she peers beyond the here and now, sensing perhaps the suffering her Son will one day undergo?

She holds Jesus firmly but gently. He meanwhile, portrayed as a chubby toddler, looks away from her, his hands resting gently on her. His relationship with her is trusting and close. He doesn't need to grasp her to seek her attention: he can take her love for granted. The straightness of his back suggests his inner strength. He is happy in his mother's embrace, but ready and prepared to respond to his Father's calling and mission.

The nakedness of Jesus emphasises the humanity of Jesus. He was truly one of us as well as divine: true God and true Man.

Though neither their eyes nor hands meet the bond between mother and son seems to have its origins in eternity.

Christ in the House of His Parents

John Everett Millais
(1829–96)
1849–50, 86.4 x 139.7 cm.
The Tate Gallery, London

Artistic Background

Millais was, like Holman Hunt, one of a group of seven British artists who wanted to recover what they thought was the purity of art before the Renaissance painter, Raphael (the pre-Raphaelites). They sought to do this by choosing clear lines and colours, simple rather than grandiose subjects and detailed realism. Millais used real models for this picture and painted sheep and tools from observation. In fact, the painting was criticised precisely because it portrayed the Holy Family in such a down-to-earth way. The symbolism is elaborate and has been said to attempt to capture some of the "mystic harmonies that beat above sense and sight" (Blake). The medium is oil on canvas.

Biblical Background

(eg. Luke 2:41-52; Matthew 13:53-58)
There is no record of the particular incident Millais portrays in the Gospels, but he uses his imagination to portray Jesus' childhood in the household of a carpenter and to explore a range of biblical themes. Assuming a knowledge of theology and church history, he refers, among other things, to the death of Jesus, the Trinity, John the Baptist and the flock of Jesus Christ. The only biblical record of an incident in Jesus' boyhood concerns his visit to the temple with his parents.

Reflecting on the Painting

The scene is a carpenter's workshop. The wood, tools, shavings and bench are painted, as are the characters, with almost photographic precision.

The boy Jesus has had an accident: he has cut the palm of his hand on a nail in the door which is being made. His mother and Joseph comfort him and the other characters all focus their attention on him. It is at this point in reflecting on the picture that the layers of meaning become apparent. The boy on the right bringing the water to bathe the cut is surely the cousin of Jesus, John the Baptist. The blood from the hand has dripped on to the foot of Jesus, prefiguring his crucifixion when his hands and feet will have nails driven through them.

Immediately above Jesus is a dove representing the Holy Spirit (this is one of the commonest devices in Christian painting) and the triangle must be a representation of the Trinity.

Outside, a flock of sheep looks on, the green of the field and blue of the sky drawing attention to them by way of contrast. If they are the flock for whom Jesus the Good Shepherd is to die, might not the bench and door represent a communion table? In this case the workshop might stand for the inside of a church; the wall would be a screen and the flock would represent the congregation. Given the painstaking symbolism it would be hard to rule out anything like this.

Some, including Charles Dickens, found all this too much, but the combination of Joseph's varicose veins, the wrinkles on Mary's forehead, and the rich symbolism, provides a way of beginning to integrate the humanity and divinity of Jesus, and to consider his family relationships.

"And Jesus grew in wisdom and stature, and in favour with God and men."

Christ among the Doctors

Bernardino Luini

(c.1481–1532)
After 1512, 72.4 x 85.7 cm.
National Gallery, London

Artistic Background

Based in Milan, and a contemporary of Leonardo da Vinci's, Luini imitated and was influenced by the great artist so much that some of his works were for a time thought to be Leonardo's. His own style, in so far as it can be seen as original, was popular and lighthearted with attractive colouring. This picture, while hanging in the Barberini gallery in Rome, was attributed to Leonardo, and could well be based on a work of his. Christ is portrayed as an ideal, other-worldly figure so beloved by the master painter. His size, which is bigger than the laws of perspective would call for, indicated his importance. This was a convention of the time.

Biblical Background

(Luke 2:41-42)
When Jesus was twelve years old his parents took him to Jerusalem to celebrate the Passover. Unbeknown to them he stayed on after they had set off back home to Nazareth. He had stayed in the temple area listening to rabbis and asking them questions. His understanding amazed those present. When his parents found him he tried to explain to them that he had to stay, because he was doing his Heavenly Father's business.

Reflecting on the Picture

Luini has simplified the whole story, and focuses on Christ and four of the rabbis. The pairs of teachers complement each other either side of him. There is a contrast between their age and his youth, between their anxiety and his serenity, and between their covered heads and his open face. The white highlighted on the clothes of Jesus reveals his purity. The blue of Jesus' sleeves is striking too, because it contrasts with the reds and pinks dominant in their clothing.

"Everyone who heard him was amazed at his understanding and his answers."

This blue indicates his royalty and is accompanied by a breastplate that has echoes of the priestly ephod. The cross-shaped straps are, of course, a representation of the death Jesus will die. His face and gaze are tinged with a sadness that suggests his foreknowledge of the death he must die in order to fulfil the many prophecies of the Scriptures: he is to be the Messiah, the Son of Man and the Suffering Servant. Does the way he points to the middle finger of his left hand refer to these three roles from the Old Testament, all of which find fulfilment in him? Or is he perhaps linking the three days Jonah spent in the belly of the great fish with his resurrection?

Whatever the meaning of this particular symbol, the whole shows one who, at the age of twelve, is already distinct from the religious leaders of his time. They are amazed at what he says but have not understood who he is. The figure gazing at us alongside Christ seems to represent a world unable to comprehend either his mission or his divinity.

The Baptism of Christ

Piero della Francesca

(c.1410–92)
1448–50, 167.5 x 116 cm.
National Gallery, London

Artistic Background

Although Piero lived a rather secluded and uneventful life in Italy his influence on European painting has been profound. Cézanne, in particular, was drawn to his insights. He was a mathematician and expressed a fondness for proportion, symmetry and congruence in his paintings. Everything and every figure is carefully conceived and placed to form a balanced whole. There is a sense of order in all he does whether in colour, shape or even abstract space. Some have seen this reflecting a spirituality in which visual order represents the essential unity of God's world seen through the eyes of faith. The medium is tempera on a panel.

Biblical Background

(Matthew 3:13-17)
John the Baptist, a cousin of Jesus (Luke 1:26ff.). was a prophet who preached the need for repentance and the forgiveness of sins. Many were drawn by his dramatic teaching and simple lifestyle, wondering if he might be the Messiah. But John was clear that his primary role was to prepare the way for the Messiah and to point people to Him. When Jesus arrived at the River Jordan, John did just this and was surprised when Jesus, the sinless one, asked to be baptised by him. In this way Jesus identified with ordinary sinful human beings, but the occasion was one when the divinity of Jesus was revealed.

Reflecting on the Painting

As we might expect from Piero the picture is both perfectly clear and yet rich in meaning and allusion. Jesus is baptised by John in an attitude of prayer, and the dove, symbolising the Holy Spirit, is central to the scene. The tree beside Jesus, symbolising both the Tree of Life in the garden of Eden and the cross, is significant in several ways. It divides the painting into two areas – on the left side are three angels; on the right are some human figures. It dominates as the cross (or tree) will dominate the life of Christ. It provides a cathedral-like form indicating the importance of the church. The River Jordan has been miraculously stopped so that Jesus stands on dry land. This recalls the occasion when the people of Israel walked across the Jordan into the Promised Land. Behind John another candidate for baptism represents every person and reinforces the identification of Jesus with believers. This figure is flanked by oriental figures who probably represent the wise men of the nativity story and also the kings mentioned in Psalm 72.

To the left of the tree the angels are like the Trinity in both diversity and yet unity. Their position also suggests a wedding: significantly in some church liturgies the wedding of Cana of Galilee falls very close to Epiphany. 'Epiphany' means the showing forth of Jesus' special mission and power, something which the wedding, the adoration of the Magi and the baptism all do. The expression of the middle figure shows a surprise that Jesus should be so identified with humanity. The one nearest the tree looks at us with a sadness that foresees the cross.

Yet there are all the signs of hope. It is a spring-time picture permeated by delicate silvery colours. In the foreground are a variety of medicinal herbs, and almost too small to see is a hint of the heavenly city, the new Jerusalem, between Christ and the tree of life. The scene is pure Umbria, which Piero paints with loving detail, but it allows universal meaning and allusions.

If it were not for the architectural-type structure of the picture such diverse and rich imagery would tend to pull it apart. In fact nothing detracts from the focus of the event, and everything enhances the meaning of this defining moment in the life of Jesus Christ.

"At that moment heaven was opened, and he saw the Spirit of God descending like a dove and alighting on him."

The Marriage at Cana

Mattia Preti
(1613–1699)
c.1660, 203.2 x 226 cm.
National Gallery, London

Artistic Background

Preti travelled widely and painted with versatility, including frescoes, ceiling canvases and altar pieces. His painting of people draws from nature, thus portraying the miracle as a real or tangible event (as distinct from something stylised and symbolic). His sense of light and dark allows him to highlight aspects of the events, faces, expressions and gestures. By choosing a scene of twenty-three or more characters he is able to portray a range of reactions to the miracle. His sense of colour and shade creates a sense of unity and balance which enhances the careful construction of the assembly around the table. The painting is on canvas.

Biblical Background
(John 2:1-10)

This was the first of the miracles of Jesus recorded in John's gospel. When the wine ran out at the wedding feast his mother Mary directed the servants to Jesus. He told them to fill six huge stone jars with water, and to draw some out, and to present it to the chief steward. When he tasted it he found the water had become wine better than any served so far in the feast. Because John is so careful with the placing of his stories and their meaning, this miracle has been seen as a prefiguration of the Lord's Supper, and also as an expression of how the old dispensation or covenant was being replaced by the new.

Reflecting on the Painting

Preti has chosen the moment when the last jar is being filled with water and the chief steward is being served the first glass of the miraculous wine. Mary, beside Jesus at the right side of the picture, gazes with a serenity, her inclined head recalling many representations of her as his mother. She is not surprised. Jesus indicates to the servants what must be done. The servant in the foreground grasps the water jar while he looks alertly at the wine being poured into the glass. The pouring of water and wine is done in a parallel way. The chief steward, highlighted in scarlet, is the first to receive the new wine, while the bride, dressed splendidly, notes intently what is happening. Meanwhile, the bridegroom and others around the far end of the table are still unaware of the miracle taking place. An empty plate and container emphasise the problem that confronted the chief steward of the wedding. Beside Jesus, one, whom we presume is a disciple or follower, has seen the truth. His hands and face express his wonder and amazement. Thus we are drawn right round the table, from the red of the steward to the blues of Jesus and Mary.

"His mother said to the servants: 'Do whatever he tells you.'"

As we continue to study the picture we notice the foot of the steward, and the dog, homely features like the bench which confirm the earthly, ordinary nature of the setting of the feast. There are no lightning flashes or angels, and yet Preti shows the dawning awareness of a miracle. Jesus does not dominate the scene by his size, actions or position and yet we keep coming back to him. We behold his glory even as we realise that it is not given to all to recognise him as Lord and God.

The Penitent Magdalen

Georges de la Tour
(1593–1652)
134 x 92 cm.
Metropolitan Museum, New York

Artistic Background

La Tour spent his whole life in France and received recognition at the highest levels of French society during his lifetime. He was, however, virtually forgotten until 1915. This picture is typical of much of his output on account of the dramatic use of a single artificial light and his preference for the colours red, yellow and brown. The influences of Caravaggio and Honthorst have been suggested for obvious reasons, but it is possible that his style, especially his use of chiaroscuro, is original. The medium is oil on canvas.

Biblical Background
(cf. Luke 7:36-50)

The rôle of Mary Magdalen(e) in the life of Jesus was an important but enigmatic one. It has been the subject of much speculation. She was healed by Jesus and went on to be one of his closest and most courageous followers. She accompanied him to the cross, was present at his burial, and was the first to see the risen Lord and to tell others of the Resurrection. The traditional association of her with a prostitute, which forms the basis of this painting, is without any biblical basis. It is possible that she anointed Jesus with oil in her home town of Magdala. It is the forgiveness of her sins, received from Jesus, that is central to an understanding of the painting.

"Therefore, I tell you, her many sins have been forgiven—for she loved much. But he who has been forgiven little loves little."

Reflecting on the Painting

This picture does not seek to portray an external event or part of the biblical narrative (i.e. Mary anointing the feet of Jesus or seeking to touch him in the garden). Rather it represents the inner spiritual conversion of Mary. For these reasons all inessentials are stripped away.

In pouring her precious oil or spices over Jesus, Mary may well have signalled the end of her prostitution, for such perfumes were the tools of her trade. Now she sits, having taken off all her jewellery, obviously at peace. Her whole demeanour: her posture, hair, hands and feet, speaks of an inner tranquillity. Her hands rest on a skull that represents her old life and nature. The past is now over, as if she had died with Christ in baptism.

She gazes at the mirror which reflects the candle-light. She isn't looking at her own reflection. The light surely stands for the light of Christ which shines in the darkness and the reflection is a reminder of the fact that we can only reflect (rather than create) light, beauty and truth.

But to look at the separate elements of the picture tends towards allegory. What de la Tour does is to create a whole out of one moment of Mary's life. The candle-light unifies each part by shadow and by highlight. The red of Mary's skirt, the crimson colour of sin, is set against the white of her blouse which is both lit and penetrated by the light, revealing an inner purity.

It is a particular insight into the penitence and conversion of Mary, but it is also a timeless portrayal of the work of grace in a fallen world.

Christ on the Lake of Gennesaret

Eugene Delacroix
(1798–1863)
c.1853, 50.8 x 61 cm.
Metropolitan Museum, New York

Artistic Background

Delacroix was born into a revolutionary situation in France, but it was not until he had visited northern Africa that his imagination caught fire. Though he reflected painstakingly on the literary background to his subject and was an art critic and draughtsman, his object was to create a moment of great drama and intensity and to involve us in it. We are to share the emotions of the story. One of the ways he does this is in his use of colours, which combine to make a graphic whole. His brushwork using oil on canvas is strong and direct. A photographer, he realised the crucial rôle for the imagination in any work of art.

Biblical Background
(Luke 8:22-25)

Jesus and his disciples set out by boat to cross Lake Gennesaret (or Galilee). Jesus fell asleep, and when a squall threatened to overwhelm the small craft he had to be awakened by his followers. They were terrified, fearing that they might drown. He got up, rebuked the wind and waves, asking the disciples what had become of their faith. They in turn were astonished that the elements obeyed him.

Reflecting on the Picture

Delacroix has chosen the moment in the story when Jesus is still asleep in the stern of the boat and the terrified disciples are about to wake him up. They are about to be engulfed in disaster. The boat is so low in the water as it lumbers towards us that a single wave could sink it. The disciple at the tiller is straining to hold the boat steady but another disciple has just lost his oar and his lurch to try to retrieve it is putting everyone in jeopardy. A disciple hugs the prow of the boat while the violent wind catches the garments of those trying to sit up.

"Who is this? He commands even the winds and the water, and they obey him."

The shore they have left looks ominously black and they clearly cannot turn back. How far the shore to which they are heading is we do do not know.

There is plenty of graphic detail but the whole mood of the story is set by the colours. The reds of the sky help to accentuate the green-white of the water in the foreground, while the boat is a solid mass of shades of red and brown. The blue of the cloak of Jesus distinguishes him from the others as much as his serenity. Given this solidarity, the supreme irony and sadness of the scene is that though Jesus is with them in the boat and shares a common destiny, every one of them is so overwhelmed by the situation that they neither look at him nor each other. Their individual panic means that they have taken their eyes off him and do not trust him. For if there had been real danger would he not have dealt with it?

Because we are drawn into the turmoil of the disciples it becomes a question for us, and given the ferocity of the weather and the state of the boat, our trust in Jesus also is put to the test at the limits.

57

The Transfiguration

Raphael (Raffaello Sanzio)
(1483–1520)
1518–20, 405 x 278 cm.
Vatican Museum, Rome

Artistic Background

This is the last of Raphael's oil paintings. It was commissioned for the Cathedral of Narbonne in France as an altar-piece, where it was intended as a companion to Sebastiano's 'Raising of Lazarus.' After his death Cardinal de Medici decided to keep it on the high altar of S. Pietro in Rome and a copy was sent to Narbonne. The medium of oil allowed a depth of shadow and richness of colour that was not possible with fresco, and marked a deliberate return to the style of Leonardo da Vinci, whose works Raphael saw when he first came to Florence.

Biblical Background
(Luke 9:28-45)

After Peter acknowledged that Jesus was the Messiah, or Christ, Jesus took him together with James and John up a mountain where his appearance changed and his clothes became bright. Moses and Elijah appeared, talking with Jesus. A voice from a cloud confirmed this was God's own Son. Meanwhile down below the other disciples had been unable to heal a boy with seizures or an evil spirit. Jesus' first act after his transfiguration was to heal the boy and return him to the care of his father.

Reflecting on the Painting

In combining two events recorded in the Gospels Raphael is able to show their very deep thematic links. The vision of Peter, James and John confirms the divinity of Jesus. He transcends the earth and is accompanied not only by Elijah holding a scroll and Moses holding the tables of the law, but by a divine

"As he was praying, the appearance of his face changed, and his clothes became as bright as a flash of lightning."

brightness. There are echoes of Raphael's 'Vision of Ezekiel.' The two figures on the left (not mentioned in the biblical account), may be saints to whom Narbonne was dedicated.

Below this majestic portrait of Jesus Christ there is a scene of frantic emotion and drama. The disciples on the left of the group, one grasping the Scriptures, are desperately trying to diagnose the boy's condition and probably to ascertain who's fault (or sin) it was. The boy's mother, father and friends are pleading for help. The arrangement of the figures means we are in a turmoil as we look at the picture. The boy's wild eyes and his right arm, together with those of two disciples and a man behind him, point to Jesus. The disciples cannot see the glory of Christ but they are indicating that this is where he is. The structure is finely arranged with Jesus at the apex of a triangle. There is no earthly solution: it lies with Jesus, God's Son. Returning to him we notice his outstretched hands – perhaps in blessing; perhaps anticipating the cross. Meanwhile the sun sets over what may well be Jerusalem, where Jesus' destiny as Saviour lies, and through whose wounds we are healed.

There is a sense of completeness in this picture, as if all Raphael's understanding and skill at the end of his life is translated onto one canvas where Old Testament and New Testament, earth and heaven, divinity and humanity meet. The care and skill with which every face and garment is painted suggests an artist at the height of his powers working with commitment and even devotion to his subject.

Kitchen Scene with Christ in the House of Martha and Mary

Diego Velasquez
(1599–1660)
1618, 60 x 103.5 cm.
National Gallery, London

Artistic Background

The special contribution of the Spaniard, Velasquez, to the history of art may well be his understanding of humanity, everyday events and ordinary life. By a brilliant use of colour and study of relationships of figures and forms, material things become vehicles or signs of something beyond. He paints direct from nature, but uses his imagination to re-cast ideas and stories to ponder on events from unique and unexpected angles. His painting of Jesus, Martha and Mary is, for example, framed as a picture and placed within another scene, enabling him to make links between a biblical narrative and contemporary life. The medium is oil on canvas.

"Martha, Martha, ... you are worried and upset about many things, but only one thing is needed.'"

Biblical Background
(Luke 10:38-42)

The home of Martha and Mary in Bethany was one of Jesus' favourite stopping places. Just outside Jerusalem, it had a peace and quiet seemingly unaffected by the bustle and political upheaval of its great neighbouring city. In the home Martha was usually the one who did the lion's share of the domestic chores and preparation, while Mary, the visionary, was prepared to sit at the feet of Jesus listening to his teaching. This so annoyed Martha that she entreated Jesus to tell Mary to help her. He responded by reminding her that "only one thing is needed." Mary is typical of the contemplative, and Martha of the active, life.

Reflecting on the Picture

The picture within a picture is painted with stark economy: the bare room has a table with a jug or plate on it. Jesus is seated and framed by a door; Mary gazes up at him, while Martha interrupts. This scene occupies a fraction of the whole canvas. The 'real picture' seems to be of a reluctant domestic servant being urged by an older woman to note the example or teaching of Jesus. There is sympathy in her posture and gentleness in her approach. The young woman is looking at us, and away from Jesus, with a hint of petulance or resentment as she continues her task with pestle and mortar. On the table before her are two garlics, four fish and two eggs, all beautifully and carefully painted, their colours and brightness a striking contrast with the sombre nature and form of the rest of the painting. The textures and uniqueness of such common cooking ingredients are thus accentuated.

And so the insights of the painting begin to reveal themselves. Neither Martha or Mary are 'right' in their usual priorities. At this moment in the biblical narrative they both come to Jesus: that is what is needed. The servant girl meanwhile has a task to do: mundane like Martha's, but in doing it she is doing the one thing necessary, and through this act she comes closer to Jesus. The material is not set against the spiritual, nor the contemplative life against the active. There is an inclusive and tender approach that befits a painting where Jesus is surrounded by four women in two ordinary homes. The knowledge of God can be found in daily work and common tasks as well as in visions or spiritual revelations.

A Parable: Return of the Prodigal Son

Rembrandt Van Rijn
(1606–69)
257 x 197.5 cm.
Hermitage Museum, St. Petersburg

Artistic Background

Rembrandt painted dozens of self-portraits, all of them revealing an honesty and self-scrutiny of almost unbearable intensity. He also painted 160 biblical themes (in addition to about 700 drawings and etchings) and he brought to them a similar desire to get to the core elements of a narrative or relationship. His use of 'chiaroscuro' (dramatic use of light and dark) heightens the contrasts, for he is able to focus attention on a particular face, gesture or feature. Rembrandt's determination to paint with integrity meant he was the first artist to draw a Jewish Jesus. The biblical characters were real people, but the stories had contemporary relevance (the clogs in this picture make a vital link). Without theatrical gestures or movements he is able to "look straight into the human heart" (Gombrich).

Biblical Background
(Luke 15:11-32)

Jesus told the story of two sons. The younger insisted on being given his inheritance. He then spent it all irresponsibly. When he was starving he came to his senses and decided to go back home to ask to work as a servant. His father however received him with open arms and celebrated his return: "For this son of mine was dead and is alive again; he was lost and is found." The older son took a dim view of the whole episode. He was angry and refused to join in the celebration, for he had stayed at home with his father, working hard, and could not find it in himself to forgive his brother's prodigality.

Reflecting on the Painting

Rembrandt has chosen the pivotal moment of the whole story. The prodigal son kneels down and rests his head against his father. He is dishevelled, his clogs are worn and his clothes are torn. The father enfolds him as he stoops gently and the tilt of his head and the light embrace all demonstrate his understanding and sympathy. His red cloak adds an ecclesiastical symbolism to the welcome, for blood-red is the colour of forgiveness. The son is not only received but forgiven. The relationship between the two could hardly be closer: they form a single unit in the structure of the picture.

But this is not the whole story.

To the right stands the older son, straight and unyielding. His staff emphasises judgement and disapproval. His face, deliberately highlighted, is impassive. He is equally distant from father and son.

This distance is further emphasised by the seated figure – a foreman at the farm perhaps, who is obviously intrigued, perhaps even moved, by the father's welcome and the young son's plight. It is he who will be responsible for organising the celebration and it will be hard, if not impossible, to bridge the gulf in the family.

Meanwhile, two shadowy figures appear in the background. One is a woman. The other looks at us. Does he bear a resemblance to Rembrandt himself, or is he the figure of Christ? We don't know, but he is looking at the viewer. His presence involves the viewer and seems to be inviting a comment or response. Perhaps he is asking which of the figures we recognise ourselves in.

> *"Let us have a feast and celebrate. For this son of mine was dead and is alive again; he was lost and is found."*

Christ Driving the Traders from the Temple

'El Greco' (Domenikos Theotokopoulos)
(1541–1614)
106.3 x 129.7 cm.
National Gallery, London

Artistic Background

The unusual effects achieved by El Greco make much of his work instantly recognisable. With creative daring he combines elements of very different traditions to form paintings full of colour, movement and classic figures. His sense of energy, also evidenced elsewhere, is particularly apparent and appropriate in this picture. He may have been drawn to this story because he understood the powerful intensity of Christ's actions, for he returned to it several times. The use of architecture behind Christ to deepen the space is typical of Tintoretto, one of his mentors, and the flowing and dynamic composition may well draw from the work of Michelangelo.

Biblical Background
(Mark 11:15-18)

The day after he arrived at Jerusalem for the climax of his ministry, Jesus entered the temple precincts. As usual the temple courts were busy with activity associated with temple worship and sacrifices. In what he had termed, "my Father's house" when a boy, he put a stop to the buying and selling by overturning tables and benches and preventing others entering. "My house will be called a house of prayer for all nations," he said, quoting Isaiah. The religious leaders began seeking a way to kill him because of his large following.

"Is it not written, 'My house will be called a house of prayer for all nations'? But you have made it a den of robbers."

Reflecting on the Picture

Jesus is central to the picture in every way. His body, elongated in typical El Greco manner, is the vertical axis of a scene of anxious movement either side. His head is framed by an arch and the temple pillars, with the sky and buildings outside performing the function of a halo. The reds and pinks of his dress are distinctive because of the contrasting range of colour elsewhere. Though balanced on one leg and about to strike a blow with his whip, his head is poised and focused.

Around Jesus the signs of his dramatic action are depicted with bodies, limbs, baskets and a table all awry. To his right the general movement is away from him – the limbs especially form very clear lines. To his left the movement is quite different – a woman walks towards the scene and others discuss the meaning of his action. In this way El Greco signals the two main elements of the story: the interruption of the buying and selling, and the beginning of the plan to kill him.

In case we have not understood this, two relief sculptures either side of Jesus spell out the point. To his right Adam and Eve are expelled from the garden of Eden, as Jesus is expelling the traders; to his left Abraham is about to sacrifice Isaac, a foreshadowing of the imminent death of Jesus. Jesus stands, therefore, both at the centre of the picture, and also at the centre of the biblical story and at the intersection of the material/secular and spiritual/religious worlds. And he is moving irresistibly towards us.

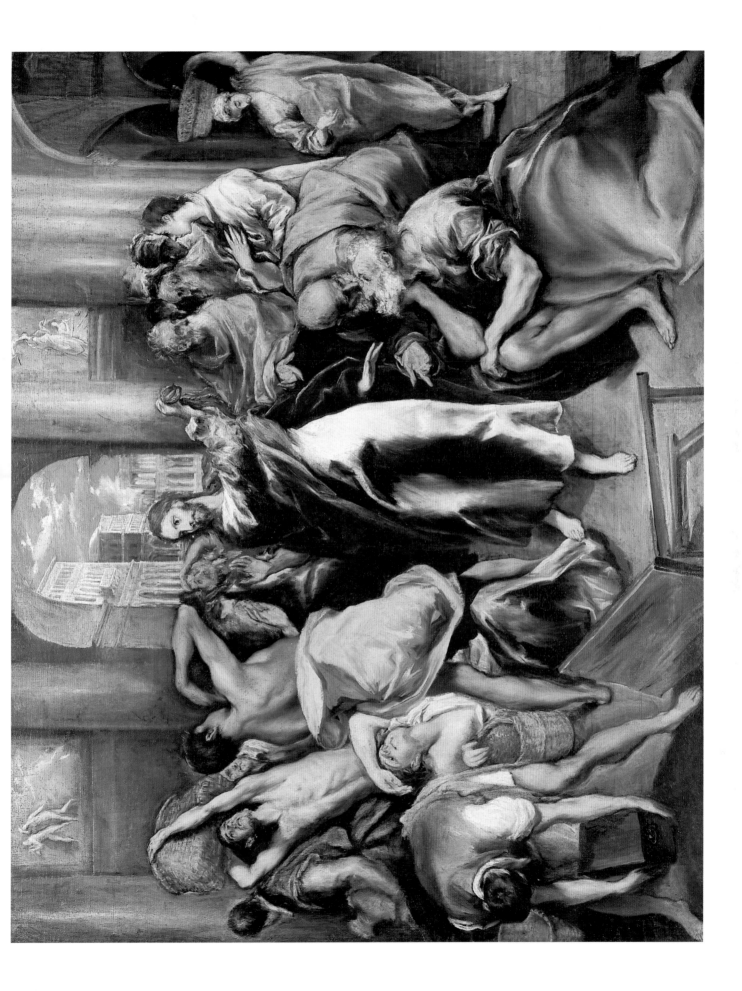

The Last Supper

Leonardo da Vinci
(1452–1519)
1495–8, 418 x 904.5 cm.
Santa Maria Della Grazie, Milan

Artistic Background

Leonardo's genius is displayed in more fields of study and endeavour than almost anyone else who lived. His painting was informed by an understanding of mathematics, philosophy, architecture, engineering, sculpture, science and music! This scene is a fresco designed to cover a monastic refectory. It was painted some way up the wall because there was a door below it (see the centre below the table). This gave Leonardo the task of altering the perspective to make the spectator seem on a level with Jesus. It is helpful to know that the disciples from the left of the picture are Bartholomew, James the Less, Andrew, Judas, Peter and John. On the right hand side continuing from Jesus are Thomas, James the Great, Philip, Matthew, Thaddeus and Simon.

Biblical Background
(Matthew 26:20-30)

Jesus and his twelve disciples had gathered in an upper room to celebrate the Passover. Jesus turned this meal into a symbol of the new covenant by saying, "Take eat: this is my body," and by calling the wine, "my blood which is shed for the remission of sins." Afterwards would come Gethsemane, the trials and his death. This symbolic act was combined with the revelation that one of the twelve was to betray Jesus. As they examined themselves Jesus said: "He that dippeth his hand with me in the dish, the same shall betray me." Immediately Judas would leave the gathering to contact the Jewish authorities and inform them of the whereabouts of Jesus.

"While they were eating, Jesus took bread, gave thanks and broke it, and gave it to his disciples."

Reflecting on the Painting

The picture is full of hidden depths. Perhaps, like the monks for whom it was intended, the viewer should return to it day by day. Among the many aspects on which to focus are: the four groups of disciples and their relationships; the character of each disciple as revealed by his face; their gestures; the knife in Peter's right hand perhaps prefiguring his act of defiance during the arrest of Jesus when he attacked one of the High Priest's retinue; Thomas, who seems to be demanding proof with his raised index finger, yet inadvertently also points heavenwards. Leonardo has given such attention to detail it is possible to study each person as if he were a separate portrait.

The character and intentions of Judas are apparent from the context. He is in shadow because he has been cut off from the light of the windows. He is alone with his secret and this is intensified by the closeness of Peter and John. His left hand, which is dipping into a plate, confirms his identity.

But, of course, the centre of attention is Jesus himself. His hands are outstretched blessing the bread and wine and his slightly inclined face is a study in sadness and resignation. He understands all things and as the Lamb of God is ready for the final sacrifice of his mission. But he is God made flesh, so the significance of this moment in time is immense. Whatever the disciples are taking in, none of them have sounded the depths of love divine compressed into this painting.

As the monks ate their own food this moving scene imbued daily routine with a divine presence, for like Leonardo they were seeking to obey the command: "Do this in remembrance of me," in their daily vocation.

The Agony in the Garden

'El Greco' (Domenikos Theotokopoulos)
(1541–1614)
102 x 131 cm.
National Gallery, London. (Copy of the original in the Museum of Art, Toledo, Ohio.)

Artistic Background

El Greco (the Greek) was actually a Spanish painter born in Crete. He was trained first in the tradition of Byzantine icons, before becoming a pupil of Titian. This combination makes his work strikingly unique. He seeks an inward expression and simplicity, yet responds to rhythm and movement. His use of colour and light verges on the daring. His rhythms are like flames and his world seems weightless. There is the fusion of the emotional qualities of the subject and of the design itself.

Though he does not lose touch with the solidity and reality of earth the human figures are caught up in another dimension. He is preoccupied with the spiritual world. It is perhaps only in the twentieth century that his creative genius has been fully appreciated. The medium is oil on canvas.

Biblical Background
(Luke 22:39-46)

Jesus had celebrated the Last Supper with his disciples. Judas had set in train the events leading up to his arrest. The normal route Jesus took from Jerusalem to Bethany (where he stayed) was over the Mount of Olives, the site of the Garden of Gethsemane. Here he asked Peter, James and John to watch and pray while he himself talked with his Father. While they slept and the soldiers prepared to arrest him, he entered into a titanic battle of will and spirit: "Father if you are willing take this cup from me; yet not my will but yours be done." An angel from heaven appeared to him and strengthened him.

"Father, if you are willing, take this cup from me; yet not my will, but yours be done."

Reflecting on the Painting

If the colour and pattern of the picture are studied before any detail or narrative, it becomes apparent that this is a scene of agonising conflict. The clouds and rocks swirl like a stormy, wave-tossed sea. The use of light and dark and a range of dramatically different colours heighten the effect. In this turmoil of competing forms and shades Jesus looks up. His friends are asleep, having understandably retreated into a womb-like state on account of tiredness and fear. Jesus has his back to the betrayer, the party of soldiers and the ghostly moon. The human experiences of doubt, fear and aloneness are accentuated by the rugged landscapes, the furtive enemies and the sleeping friends.

The angel comes to comfort him in his hour of greatest need holding a cup. It is no opium or morphine but the cup of suffering: the cup of God's will. The symbol is used frequently by the Old Testament prophets. The angel brings strength not by taking Jesus out of the shadow of death, but by confirming that this is the Father's will. His death at the hands of fearful, jealous, resentful, sinful people is inevitable unless he denies who and what he is. A ray of light from Heaven brings echoes of the baptism and transfiguration of Jesus. His face reveals the deep sadness of the hour, but in and through it all he is at peace. How El Greco conveys that stillness remains a mystery, reflecting the depths and mystery of that lonely vigil in the garden.

Christ before the High Priest

Gerrit (Gerhard) van Honthorst
1592–1656
c.1617, 272 x 183 cm.
National Gallery, London

Artistic Background

Honthorst was a Dutch artist who was very popular in the courts of Europe. Although his works may seem representational and unexceptional to modern eyes, in their own time they were revolutionary. Following Caravaggio, he painted directly from models and observation. Like Caravaggio he also used artificial lighting to heighten the dramatic effect of his work. In fact, due to his use of light and dark he was nicknamed 'Gherardo delle Notti' (Gerhard of the night). The canvas is lifesize and this scale is vital in understanding the powerful effect the picture has on the viewer. The medium is oil.

Biblical Background

(See Matthew 26:57-68)
Jesus had been arrested in Gethsemane at night. His popularity with the crowds meant it was not politically expedient during the day time. The religious leaders were determined to have him put to death. To this end a 'trial' was hastily arranged during the night before Caiaphas the high priest. No reliable evidence or witnesses were forthcoming and so two false witnesses were produced. They misinterpreted Jesus' teaching about his own death and resurrection (John 2:19) and claimed he was talking about literally destroying and rebuilding the temple. Caiaphas sought a response and stands up in his frustration. When Jesus remained silent he demanded: "Tell us if you are the Christ, the Son of God." "Yes, it is as you say," replied Jesus. This was enough for those present to conclude that Jesus was worthy of death. (Later they persuaded the crowd and Pilate to demand the crucifixion of Jesus, the Christ.)

Reflecting on the Painting

Honthorst has chosen the most dramatic and pivotal moment in the trial. Caiaphas is demanding, under oath, that Jesus declares whether or not he is the Messiah, the Son of God. Behind him are the two shifty-looking witnesses. Behind Jesus are those who have arrested him, armed with weapons. But the candle at the centre of the picture draws attention to the two main figures and the contrast between them could not be greater. Caiaphas is dressed in a rich gown, Jesus is wearing a simple, torn smock; Caiaphas is seated, Jesus must stand; the finger of Caiaphas is free to point, Jesus' hands are bound; Caiaphas rests on a table and chair, Jesus has no support; Caiaphas has the backing of witnesses, Jesus has only captors behind him; Caiaphas has an open Book of the Law for reference and authority, Jesus is his own authority.

And yet as the viewer's eyes move from the face of Caiaphas to the finger, then to the face of Jesus, to the candle, and back, a deeper contrast emerges. It is Caiaphas who is worried, Jesus who is peaceful and composed; the hands of Caiaphas are anxious, the bound hands of Jesus are completely relaxed. And it isn't long before the rôles are reversed: Jesus is the one who is asking the real question. He is looking into the heart of Caiaphas revealing his motives, like a searchlight cutting into the darkness. In his humanity the Light of the World is revealed. Jesus is the Christ, the Son of God. The hypocrisy and duplicity of the prosecution blind them to the truth, but there is a hint that one of the soldiers might be beginning to understand who Jesus really is. By the tilt of his head and his expression it looks as if he, at least, is honest and open to the truth.

As for the quill: is it by chance it points towards Jesus, the Word become flesh? Is it there for a written confession? The barrenness of words and the Law, if so, are contrasted with the living Word. Perhaps Honthorst has left this for the viewer to decide.

"Tell us if you are the Christ, the Son of God."

Pilate Washing his Hands

Mattia Preti
(1613–99)
206 x 184.8 cm.
Metropolitan Museum, New York

Artistic Background

Also called 'Il Calabrese,' Preti was an Italian painter who travelled widely in Europe. It was through his mentor, Guercino, that the influence of the Venetian school, including Caravaggio, came. He painted religious scenes in churches in Rome, the Carthusian Chapel in Naples and also frescoes for the Cathedral at Valletta, Malta, where he lived for the last 40 years of his life. He was versatile, working in fresco, on canvas and altarpieces, and was particularly at ease with religious works exploring emotions and reactions to significant events. This work uses oil on canvas.

Biblical Background
(Matthew 27:11-26)

After the rushed 'trial' of Jesus the Jewish leaders handed him over to Pilate, the Roman governor of the province. Jesus did not defend himself against any accusations and Pilate, urged by his wife, tried to find a way of releasing Jesus. The crowd shouted, "Crucify him," and, afraid of a riot, Pilate symbolically washed his hands of the blood of Jesus, passing responsibility for his death to the crowd. He then released Barabbas and handed Jesus over to be crucified.

"When Pilate saw that he was getting nowhere, but that instead an uproar was starting, he took water and washed his hands in front of the crowd.'"

Reflecting on the Painting

As Pilate washes his hands – an act that would earn him a notorious place in history – Jesus, with a crown of thorns, is led away. He has a rope around his neck and the cross is already on its way outside the city via the Roman arches. The crowd looks on eagerly. To the left is a mysterious figure who may be Barabbas – if so he is looking at the man who died on the cross intended for him. The little negro serving boy holding the ceremonial plate gazes intently at Pilate's face, while the serving girl, having provided the water, lingers to watch this moment of history. An old soldier seems resigned and unsurprised by Pilate's decision. Perhaps he will be responsible for the execution, having guarded Barabbas to this point in time. On the other hand he may be responsible for law and order in the city of Jerusalem.

Pilate alone gazes at us with a piercing look – there is a sadness mixed with inquisitiveness, as if he is inquiring what we would have done in the same situation. In looking at us he is turning away from Jesus, but the predominant colour of the picture, red, will not let us forget that the lifeblood of Jesus is soon to be shed.

The sky itself provides a crimson background to the sad scene. Not all the water in the world could wash away the responsibility for this man's blood. But Pilate's gaze engages us. Could it be that we bear some responsibility too?

The Crucifixion

Matthias Grünewald
(1475–1528)

1516, A panel from the Isenheim Altarpiece,
Musée d'Unterlinden, Colmar, France

Artistic Background

A Bavarian, Grünewald was not directly affected by the Renaissance with its realism and humanism, yet his work displays an original and very personal vision of Christ's suffering. It was designed for the hermits of Saint Anthony who provided hospitality for the victims of the plague. As they looked at the altar-piece in their death agonies they saw another who had suffered. The pain is unremitting and in no way compromised, but its setting among the other panels offers hope. There are three groups of three panels: this central one is flanked immediately by the Virgin and Child on one side and the Resurrection on the other. This picture is one of ten painted for an altar at Isenheim.

Biblical Background

(cf. John 19:16-37 and Matthew 27:45-46) After being flogged Jesus was crucified. A notice hung above him proclaiming him to be 'Jesus of Nazareth, King of the Jews' ('INRI'). Near the cross were his mother, Mary Magdalene and John, the disciple Jesus loved. The physical, mental, emotional and spiritual agony Jesus experienced before he finally died is expressed in his cry: "My God, my God, why hast thou forsaken me?"

Reflecting on the Painting

On the left side of the cross is Mary fainting into the arms of John the Disciple. Mary Magdalene is crying over his awful fate, while at the foot of the cross stands her alabaster jar, perhaps a reminder of how she anointed Jesus at Magdala. On the other side of the cross John the Baptist, who had, of course, long since been executed, is shown pointing to the Saviour. The lamb beside him whose blood is dripping into a chalice symbolises the Lamb of God who takes away the sin of the world.

"When he had received the drink, Jesus said, 'It is finished.' With that, he bowed his head and gave up his spirit."

Nothing, however, can detract from the figure of Christ. Set against the darkness accompanying his death, his lacerated body is hoisted taut and contorted. Grünewald has understood the physical horrors of crucifixion, arguably the most cruel form of execution. Pain seems to cry out from every part of the wracked body – the legs, the torso, the shoulders, the head, the mouth, the arms and the fingers, which seem an extension or expression of the crown of thorns.

Here there is no hint of beauty or form – even the colours with dark red blood contrasting the green flesh and festering wounds are revolting. In this Grünewald is true to the narrative of the gospels and especially to the prophecies of Isaiah 53 and Psalm 22. The picture conveys a powerful terror of almost unbearable intensity.

There is no hint of resolution of the anguish in this particular piece of the altar-panel except for the size of Christ. He is out of proportion – emphasising in a typical mediaeval way his importance. The witnesses on the left-hand side of the picture see the human suffering and mourn him as man; those on the right reveal the divine intention and acclaim him as Saviour: by these wounds we are healed.

Pietà

Michelangelo (Buonarroti)

(1475–1564)

c.1498

St. Peter's, Rome

Artistic Background

Michelangelo excelled as an artist, a sculptor and an architect. His works are based on his own anatomical research, dissection and numerous studies from models. This Pietà, ('pieta' is Italian for 'pity' and came to be specifically associated with the body of Jesus in his mother's lap) was completed in response to a commission of 1498. It is the first of several and was intended to be a monument to a French cardinal. In its realism (accuracy and anatomy) and simplicity it broke new ground. One of the practical problems he solved in the sculpture was how to support a male body on female knees. He uses her garments as a podium. The work is in marble.

Biblical Background

(eg. John 19:28-42)

The relationship between Jesus and his mother forms a background to the whole of Jesus' life and ministry. The virgin birth itself puts a special gloss on the closeness and meaning of their togetherness. Jesus respected his mother throughout his childhood. His first miracle was ushered in by her trust in him. Later she sought to prevent harm coming to them because of his calling and ministry. (Mark 3:20-21). She then followed him to the cross itself (John 19:25-27) where Jesus entrusted her to John's care. The scene depicted by this sculpture is not described in the Gospels, but there is a long tradition that she recovered the dead body of her son as it was taken down from the cross for burial.

Reflecting on the Sculpture

Jesus lies relaxed and at peace. He bears the scars of the crucifixion but they do not mar the beauty of his body. Michelangelo has put all his skill into portraying the perfection of his body: his beautifully proportioned limbs, his hands and feet. There is no sign to label Jesus as the Messiah or the Son of God but his very perfect naked body invites that conclusion and expresses a spiritual dimension.

"They will look on the one they have pierced."

Mary cradles him and her flowing robes provide an embrace for him. Her right arm holds him, her left is outstretched as if seeking the meaning of his whole life and ministry. Her face is young – controversially young for the mother of a 33 year-old – and she remains serene and gracious. Perhaps she is praying rather than looking at the body of her dear son.

The wheel has come full circle. When she offered her body to bear the son who was to become the Saviour of the world it was an act of trust and obedience. Now that the seeming tragedy of his death has occurred before her eyes, she holds him again. He is equally helpless and the faith she requires is no less. She has not lost her belief that God through His Holy Spirit is working this ghastly episode into good.

So through a dead body in a mother's arms Michelangelo seeks to transcend death. This relationship and its spiritual meaning are eternal.

The Resurrection of Christ

Piero della Francesca
(c.1410–92)

1463, 225 x 205 cm.

Borgo San Selpolcro, Palazzo Communale

Artistic Background

The same sense of structure and balance exemplified in 'The Baptism of Christ' is found in this mural. The architectural-like pyramid, of which Christ forms the apex and the four soldiers the base, is carefully constructed. Another v-shape starts beneath his foot and extends via the two central soldiers, the spear and the placement of trees, mountain and branches. The perspective which places the lid of the sarcophagus out of view is subtly arranged to avoid any exploration of the question of how the risen Christ emerged from a sealed tomb. The colours are delicately chosen from pinks and shades of green and grey to form a Cézanne-like unity and balance. It is a fresco mural with tempera and has been rated one of the supreme works of art of all time.

Biblical Background
(Matthew 27:57–28:15)

In Matthew's account of the resurrection of Christ the rôle of the soldiers in guarding the body is stressed. They were to ensure that no one stole the corpse. The guards did not witness the resurrection itself, but were paid to spread the story that the disciples of Jesus stole him while they were sleeping. The wounds of Jesus were still present in his resurrection body (see John 20:19-31 and the painting by Caravaggio) yet his appearance was such that disciples and friends did not recognise him at first.

Reflecting on the Painting

The highly personal nature of this picture is perhaps underlined by the fact that the unhelmeted soldier has been taken as a self-portrait. Whether this is so or not the painting has a quite unique power and effect for many.

"You are to say, 'His disciples came during the night and stole him while we were asleep.'"

The four soldiers represent a sleeping world, unaware of the unparalleled nature of this moment in history. Not long before three of Jesus' disciples were sleeping in Gethsemane while he prayed in anguish. Now his triumph goes unwitnessed.

The weapons are irrelevant and serve only to act as a frame for the risen Christ who is Lord "of a kingdom not of this world." The flag that he holds contrasts with the spear. It unites symbolically the whole of creation, and the blood-red cross shows that the despair of Calvary has been transformed into a redeeming cause. The risen Lord is placed straight down the centre of the picture, the upright banner and his raised knee emphasising the vertical dimension in contrast to the triangles already noted. The uniqueness and central importance of Christ could hardly be more persuasively conveyed.

But it is the character of Jesus, revealed especially in his face, to which we are drawn irresistibly. It has a rugged beauty, with dark around the eyes, asymmetrical lips, a coarse beard. But combined they contribute to a devouring gaze. It is icon-like: what in the Byzantine and orthodox tradition is called a Pantocrator – a man-god, human and divine. The gaze is undeviating and uncompromising – the lack of emotion indicates perhaps the impartiality and objectivity of the One who is Judge of the living and the dead.

Yet behind the face the dawn is breaking and the clouds are tinged with light. The cold tomb, the sleeping soldiers and the dead-looking trees and shrubs are present at, though not aware of, the dawn of a new era in history in which death itself has been conquered.

Noli Me Tangere (Don't Touch Me)

Titian (Tiziano Vecelli)
(c.1487–1576)
After 1516, 108.6 x 90.8 cm.
National Gallery, London

Artistic Background

Titian is widely regarded as the most important Venetian painter of the 16th century. His reputation was as great as Michaelangelo's and he was in demand all over Europe. Influenced by Bellini and Giorgione, his style is very expressive. His portraits are notable for their revealing insight into character and motivation. He explored the great themes of love, life and death. His technique, involving layers of glazes and colours, inspired later generations of artists, especially the Impressionists. His use of colour is particularly sensitive, allowing him great subtleties of insight and feeling. Colours provide for unity and narrative, rather than formal structure.

Biblical Background

(John 20:1-18)

According to John's gospel, the first person on Easter Day to visit the tomb where Jesus was buried was Mary Magdalene. She discovered the stone had been rolled away, and that the tomb was empty. She told Simon and John, who ran to confirm her story. After they left she stayed in the garden. Jesus stood by her but she thought he was the gardener. When he called her "Mary" she realised who he was. He then told her not to touch him because he had not yet returned to his Father. She left the scene to tell the others, "I have seen the Lord."

"Jesus said to her, 'Mary.' She turned towards him and cried out in Aramaic, 'Rabboni!'"

Reflecting on the Painting

This encounter is one of the most poignant and moving in the gospel story. As the kneeling Mary reaches out Jesus withdraws his cloak, or grave-clothes, while at the same time leaning sensitively towards her. He holds a garden hoe, explaining why she assumed him to be the gardener. She rests her left hand on a container, possibly the one in which she has the ointment or spices for his dead body. He bears the scar of a nailprint in his right foot. Their figures, though not touching at any point, combine to form a beautifully elegant pattern. There is a sensuality about the painting of them both which heightens the sense of drama as this devoted woman reaches out to touch the semi-naked figure of the Saviour of the world. Their clothes are lightly textured and the contrast between the red of her overgarment and the white could hardly be stronger given the colours of the landscape in which they are set. Echoes of the scarlet standing for sin and white for purity are consciously evoked.

The background is integral to the story. The tree links their encounter to the sky and divides the picture into a pastoral scene with sheep (behind Jesus) and a village together with path and man walking a dog (behind Mary). It is a meeting not only of individuals but of cultures. The shrubs are minutely observed and painted. The sheep represent the Church which was created by the resurrection of Jesus. There is a healing implicit in the person of Jesus which seems to radiate into and infuse every part of the whole. And the daybreak is portrayed in rich colours, evoking the dawn of a new era.

The Supper at Emmaus

Michelangelo Merisi da Caravagglo
(1573–1610)
(c.1606), 141 x 196.2 cm.

Artistic Background

Caravaggio took his name from his Italian birthplace. His influence on European art has been profound. Rembrandt and Honthorst owe much to him, for example. This painting brings together nearly everything for which Caravaggio is renowned: dramatic use of light and shade (chiaroscuro); painting from real life and models; a seriousness and intensity as he focuses on a moment of great significance where all the elements of the whole combine to reveal the highly charged nature of the event.

Biblical Background
(Luke 24:13-35)

Although the tomb in which Jesus was buried was found empty on Easter day his followers were bewildered and fearful, not understanding what had happened or what it meant. Two of them left Jerusalem for a village called Emmaus. As they walked they were joined by the risen Christ but did not recognise him. They talked to him of his death and the empty tomb, at which point he chided them for not recognising how the Scriptures had come true. On arriving at Emmaus they urged him to stay with them. As he took the bread, blessed it, broke it and began to give it to them, they suddenly realised who he was. Jesus left them, and they returned immediately to tell the other disciples they had met the risen Lord.

Reflecting on the Painting

In addition to Jesus and his two followers Caravaggio has introduced an innkeeper into the picture. His face is in shade and he casts a shadow that forms the background to Jesus. The table is set and the food looks fresh and appetising. Jesus has just broken the bread into three pieces and is blessing the meal as the moment of truth dawns simultaneously on Cleopas and his friend. The innkeeper's incomprehension only confirms the way in which this disclosure is revealed rather than found by listening or searching.

Some have suggested that it was the nailprints in the hands of Jesus that gave his identity away, but Caravaggio has deliberately obscured these scars. What the single source of light highlights are the face and right hand of Jesus and the dramatic gestures and movements of the disciples. The one stretches out his arms in amazement reaching towards us in the process; the other is poised to get up and is literally on the edge of his seat.

There is no halo, none of the traditional signs of divinity or blessedness.

Everything, from the water, to the loaf, to the shell on the leather garment, is realistically portrayed, yet here is a moment of divine revelation. In a short while the innkeeper will be left alone: Jesus is about to disappear and the guests will hurry back to Jerusalem. The meal he has prepared is untouched, apart from the broken bread – and just three empty chairs will remain. What he makes of it all we are left to ponder, and of course, he represents all those of us who were not present at the cross or the tomb, but who yet seek to understand.

"Then their eyes were opened and they recognised him, and he disappeared from their sight."

The Conversion of Saul

Michelangelo (Buonarroti)
(1475–1564)
1542–5
Cappella Paolina, Rome

Artistic Background

This is the last but one of Michelangelo's paintings and is in some senses a culmination of much of his work. Forms, figures and themes are full of echoes from the past. In his later years the effects of the Reformation spread across Europe and it would be surprising had Michelangelo not been aware of its challenges to the formal hierarchy, dogmas and traditions of the Church. This picture, dealing with the conversion of an individual, is very much in touch with one of the central tenets of Reformation theology: the direct relationship between an individual and God through Jesus Christ. It is as though he was aware that the whole worldview which his work embodied, and of which it was a part, was changing. If so he was working through such implications in a painting commissioned by Pope Paul III.

"Who are you, Lord?" Saul asked. "I am Jesus, whom you are persecuting," he replied. "Now get up and go … ."

Biblical Background
(Acts 9:1-19)

After the resurrection and ascension of Christ, and the coming of the Holy Spirit at Pentecost, the early Christians experienced much persecution. One of the most zealous of their critics and persecutors was Saul, a rabbi from Tarsus. He was present when Stephen was stoned to death for his faith and even actively seeking to imprison those who were termed the "followers of the Way." On his way to Damascus with authorisation from the high priest to arrest Christians, he was sent tumbling to the ground by a light from heaven. He heard Jesus speaking to him. Those travelling with him heard the sound but could see no one. Blinded, Saul was led into Damascus where one of the Christians he had planned to arrest welcomed him.

Reflecting on the Painting

The theme of this picture is conversion and, despite its many figures in various clusters and postures, Michelangelo is single-minded in pursuit of portraying the first moment of a sinner's response to divine intervention.

The scene is divided into two realms: the heavenly and the earthly, and although Damascus is depicted on the right, this great city and its inhabitants are of no significance. The purpose of Saul's journey is now irrelevant, as is everything else, as he feels the full force of God's power.

In the biblical narrative it is Jesus who speaks to Saul, but here it is the Father who is portrayed. He is surrounded by heavenly beings all in human form. They understand and react with a sense of urgency to his intervention in the life of Saul.

On earth the scene is quite different: in place of harmony of the heavenly figures, all is terror and confusion. The horse from which Saul has been thrown seeks to bolt off; two figures on the left run away; another tries to protect himself from the light with a shield. On either side of the horse there is a group of terrified people, some with weapons or military dress reacting like a defeated army.

Saul himself lies in the foreground shielding his bearded face from the light with his arm. He is overcome by the divine presence. His eyes are closed and he is a passive recipient of whatever God directs towards him. We find ourselves witnessing a re-enactment of the creation of Adam. Then God created the first man; now he creates a new man. The sin, guilt, anger, confusion of Saul's inner world is represented by his companions. They are presented in every sort of contortion and disarray. Before the soul of Saul can respond he must first be isolated from his misguided mission in life and from all that binds him to it. Only then, and painfully so, can the great transformation take place. Everything about the painting suggests difficulty and pain. There is little joy or ease about it. This may stem from Michelangelo's penetration into the anguish of spiritual birth.

The Light of the World

Holman Hunt
(1827–1910)
1854, 121.3 x 52 cm.
Keble College, Oxford

Artistic Background

A pre-Raphaelite, like Millais, Hunt was painstaking in his attention to detail. He was saturated in the Bible and his best known works are on biblical themes. The other main version of this famous painting is in St Paul's Cathedral, London. It is one of the most popular Christian paintings among Protestants, adorning hundreds of thousands of homes, the subject of numerous hymns and choruses, and fulfilling the functions of an icon. This image of Christ, knocking at the door of the human heart, has found its way into the collective unconscious of much Evangelical theology. The medium is oil on canvas.

Biblical Background

(Revelation 3:20, John 12:46)
In the last book of the Bible Jesus is portrayed as standing at the door of the church of Laodicea: "Here I am! I stand at the door and knock. If anyone hears my voice and opens the door, I will come in and eat with him and he with me." This is linked with the description in John's Gospel of Jesus as the Light of the World. The combined images create something unique which has been applied to the encounter between Jesus and an individual soul. To this day it is replicated, as in a current U.S. recording: "Into my heart, into my heart, come into my heart, Lord Jesus."

"I have come into the world as a light, so that no one who believes in me should stay in darkness."

Reflecting on the Picture

Wherever the picture has appeared (and it has travelled all over the world) it has been accompanied by an explanation given by John Ruskin in a letter to *The Times* (May 4th, 1854).

It is possibly the best way to understand what Holman Hunt intended. The whole is meticulously constructed from a divine collection of individual biblical themes and narratives.

"The door is that of the human soul. It has never been opened. Christ approaches it in the night, dressed in robes which represent prophet (the white robe), priest, (the breastplate) and king (the crown interwoven with thorns).

"There are two lights: the first in the lantern which represents conscience – it is red and fierce and falls on the weeds cluttering the closed door and on the apple which is a reminder of the original sin of mankind. The second light comes from the head of Jesus. It represents salvation; it is subdued and soft."

Ruskin went on to say: "I think it one of the noblest works of sacred art ever produced in this or any other age." And this view has influenced many. Others have found the allegory and contrived nature of the symbolism too much. It is a sermon as much as a picture and nothing is left to chance. The hands and feet are nail-pierced; the halo (a very non-pre-Raphaelite symbol) is perhaps what explains, along with the rounded shape of the top of the picture, the icon-like effect.

The picture has functioned in the English-speaking world in the same way as great hymns (eg. 'Rock of Ages') in providing new images that shape people's understanding of the Gospel. Even if it doesn't have a powerful effect as you ponder it, it is worth studying in order to understand why it has inspired such devotion among countless Christians.

The Four Horsemen of the Apocalypse

Albrecht Dürer
(1471–1528)
1498, 39.4 x 28 cm.
Private Collection

Artistic Background

Dürer's work is hard to place in time and space, because he lived at the intersection of some of the most significant changes of all time. At Nuremberg he was aware of the very different traditions of Northern and Southern European art. When he visited Italy the revolutionary artistic ideas of Leonardo da Vinci were taking root. In Germany he came face to face with the revolutionary theological doctrines of the Reformation. Somehow he managed to hold in creative tension these very different perspectives. He was a painter, engraver, designer of woodcuts and writer on art theory. Among his most famous studies is a sketch called 'Praying Hands.' This work is one of a set of 15 woodcuts, 'The Apocalypse.'

Biblical Background

(Revelation 6:1-8; Zechariah 1:8-17, 6:1-8) The book of Revelation, so popular in late mediaeval times, is perhaps more difficult for modern readers. The imagery of the Old Testament prophets and of St. John the Divine is powerful and disturbing. Some see it pointing to the last days, or even to a period after the second coming of Christ. Others see in it a depiction of the truth in and behind history itself. The four horsemen each ride horses of different colours. The top one (right) in the picture is white; the second one, red; the third one is black and the bottom one is deathly pale.

"I looked, and there before me was a white horse! Its rider held a bow, and he was given a crown, and he rode out as a conqueror bent on conquest."

Reflecting on the Woodcut

Given that the colours of the horses and horsemen are so dominant in the source material and that Dürer in a woodcut could not use colour, the dilemma he faced was a fundamental one. His skill as a portraitist and master observer of nature meant he could overcome the problem with specific and graphic details.

The picture is full of movement, and yet has perfect balance. The top horseman is a conqueror and represents the power of those in authority; the second with brandished sword represents war; the central and dominant horseman with the seals represents famine, possibly hinting at the prevalence of scarcity and want in the world of Dürer's time. The fourth rider represents death: both he and his horse are frail, almost dead. They pursue human beings irresistibly. In the bottom left-hand corner is a grotesque monster devouring a mitred figure: is the Church itself at risk?

Above the scene, coming out of the clouds, is the angel unloosing these forces on the earth, and to the left is the sign of divine presence and glory.

In the centre foreground are Dürer's famous initials. Ironically, of course, they also stand for *Anno Domini*, a reminder, however unconsciously, of the way in which the four horsemen have continued to dominate history in spite of the coming of the Prince of Peace.

The Great Day of His Wrath

John Martin
(1789–1854)
1852, 196.5 x 303 cm.
Tate Gallery, London

Artistic Background

John Martin painted landscapes and biblical subjects at a time when the human response to nature was being revolutionalised. The Romantic movement stressed drama, feelings and emotions. In place of the neat backgrounds of earlier paintings (including many in this selection) the natural world often becomes the subject, or a very powerful element, of the painting. This huge canvas is one of three, all equally imposing. The powerful effect of each in context is difficult to portray. His brushwork is rather bland and his sense of colour may be poor, but the combination of such dominating reds and dramatic forms seems at times commensurate with the gravity and awesome nature of the subject. The medium is oil.

Biblical Background
(Revelation 6:12-17)

The Day of Wrath (or Day of the Lord) is a recurrent theme in the Old Testament prophets, and is the backcloth to some of the last teaching of Jesus (eg. Matthew 24:15-29). In Revelation the description is more graphic than anywhere else: an earthquake is followed by the sun turning black and the moon red. Stars fall to earth, the sky is rolled up and mountains are removed from their place. The survivors on earth plead with the tumbling mountains to fall on them and hide them from the wrath of God.

> *"They called to the mountains and the rocks, 'Fall on us' and hide us from the face of him who sits on the throne and from the wrath of the Lamb!"*

Reflecting on the Painting

Without the counterbalance of the other two paintings, 'The Last Judgement' and 'The Plains of Heaven,' this picture is unremittingly horrific and disturbing. Every possible artistic technique is called up to overwhelm the viewer. The figures in the foreground are distinct enough for us to identify with their impending doom and yet the perspective of the picture reaches into a blazing infinity. In between, whole families, buildings and cities on the right-hand sands collapse into an abyss, while on the left boulders of unimaginable size and menace tumble down like huge millstones to complete the crashing process. Lightning flashes and the dominant colour is a blood-red.

The whole effect recreates that of gigantic waves in a raging sea, and echoes of the fate of the Egyptian army engulfed by the Red Sea are not hard to find.

The '*Dies Irae*' has been portrayed hauntingly in music, for example, in the Verdi *Requiem*. Martin here fuses an unparalleled imaginative response to landscape with a vision of almost unbearable intensity.

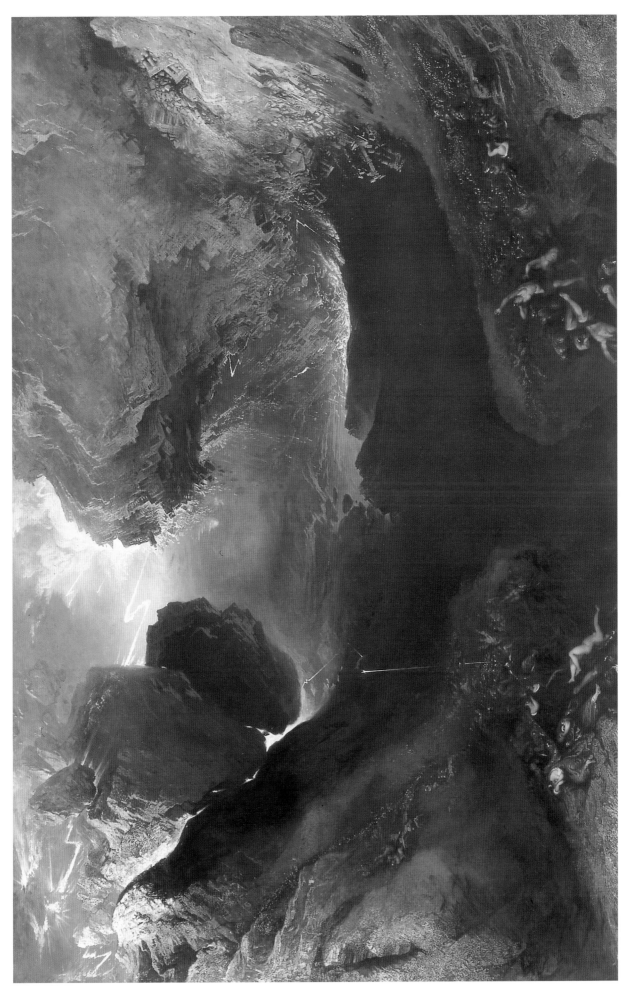

Christ in Glory in the Tetramorph

Graham Sutherland
(1903–80)
c.1960, 24 x 11.4 m.
Coventry Cathedral, England

Artistic Background

This huge tapestry, weighing three quarters of a ton and dominating the east end of Coventry Cathedral, was almost unique in the output of Sutherland, a British twentieth-century artist. Though he had painted a famous Crucifixion, he is better known for his landscapes, portraits and abstracts. It was intended by Sir Basil Spence, the architect of this modern cathedral, to communicate directly with ordinary people who worshipped there. It was Spence who specified the theme: a Christ-figure set in a tetramorph (the four creatures representing the Evangelists who wrote the gospels). Though contemporary in aspects of its style the tapestry is based on a rich tradition of symbolism; Egyptian, Romanesque, Greek and Byzantine.

Biblical Background

(See Revelation 4:1-11)

In the last book of the Bible Jesus Christ is portrayed as seated in glory surrounded by a host of creatures and elders. This tapestry singles out the four Evangelists and identifies them by their traditional symbols: a lion, Mark; a calf, Luke; a man, Matthew; and a flying eagle, John. Christ's feet are nail-pierced, a link with the crucifixion scene below which serves as a backcloth to the communion table or altar. The tapestry is symbolic of the divinity and authority of Christ; it also affirms Christ as the Lord of history.

"You are worthy ... to receive glory and honour and power ..."

Reflecting on the Tapestry

As it is virtually impossible to view the tapestry without the altar or communion table in the foreground, perhaps the best way to reflect upon it is to imagine kneeling before it to receive the bread and wine. Immediately in front of the eyes is a depiction of the crucifixion of Jesus with contorted branches emphasising the sheer pain and intensity of suffering. Above this scene, linked by a chalice, is a minute human form sheltered between two pierced feet. The seated figure of Christ in glory is surrounded in several ways including the four creatures. The contrasts between Christ and the crucifixion are dramatic, not just in scale but also in His powerful, still, gentle presence and majesty. The struggles of the creatures put into relief the massive peacefulness of Christ's presence. As the eyes reach the top of the scene the Holy Spirit hovers, radiant above everything, a visual parallel with the light throughout the cathedral. The enigmatic figure to the right is St. Michael engaged in his final battle with the Devil. It serves to reinforce the magnificent peace and completeness of the risen Christ, His authority and His victory. This is how He is now seen through the spiritual eyes of faith and how He will be seen by every eye at the end of time. Here is the fulfilment of what we first glimpsed in the creation of the world and the gift of conscious life to Adam.

Bible References to the Pictures

Old Testament

'The Ancient of Days'	William Blake	Proverbs 8:22-27; Daniel 7:9-14
The Creation of Adam	Michelangelo	Genesis 1:1–2:8
Expulsion from Paradise	Masaccio	Genesis 2:4–3:24
The Exile from the Ark and the Drunkenness of Noah	Bedford Book of Hours	Genesis 8:15–9:23
Tower of Babel	Escher	Genesis 11:1-95
Lot Fleeing with His Daughters from Sodom	Dürer	Genesis 18:20–19:38
Rebecca at the Well	Pellegrini	Genesis 24
Jacob with the Flock of Laban	Jusepe de Ribera	Genesis 30:25-43
Joseph in Egypt	Jacopa da Pontormo	Genesis 37–50
The Brazen Serpent	Tiepolo	Numbers 21:6-9; John 3:14-15
The Scapegoat	Holman Hunt	Leviticus 16
The Visit of the Queen of Sheba to King Solomon	E.J. Poynter	2 Chronicles 8:1–9:28
Vision of Ezekiel	Raphael	Ezekiel 1:1-14
The Three Men in the Fiery Furnace	Catacomb, Rome	Daniel 3
Belshazzar's Feast	Rembrandt	Daniel 5

New Testament

The Madonna del Granduca	Raphael	Matthew 1:18-25; 2:1-12; Luke 2:1-7
Christ in the House of his Parents	Millais	Matthew 13:53-58
Christ among the Doctors	Bernardino Luini	Luke 2:41-52
The Baptism of Christ	Piero della Francesca	Matthew 3:13-17
The Marriage at Cana	Mattia Preti	John 2:1-10
The Penitent Magdalen	Georges de la Tour	Luke 7:36-50
Christ on the Lake of Gennesaret	Delacroix	Luke 8:22-25
The Transfiguration	Raphael	Luke 9:28-45
Kitchen Scene with Christ in the Home of Martha and Mary	Velazquez	Luke 10:38-42
A Parable: Return of the Prodigal Son	Rembrandt	Luke 15:11-32
Christ Driving the Traders from the Temple	El Greco	Mark 11:15-18
The Last Supper	Leonardo da Vinci	Matthew 26:20-30
The Agony in the Garden	El Greco	Luke 22:39-46
Christ before the High Priest	Honthorst	Matthew 26:57-68
Pilate Washing his Hands	Mattia Preti	Matthew 27:11-26
The Crucifixion	Grünewald	John 19:16-37; Matthew 27:45-46
Pietà	Michelangelo	John 19:28-42
The Resurrection of Christ	Piero della Francesca	Matthew 27:57–28:15
Noli Me Tangere (Don't Touch Me)	Titian	John 1:1-18
The Supper at Emmaus	Caravaggio	Luke 24:13-35
The Conversion of Saul	Michelangelo	Acts 9:1-19
The Light of the World	Holman Hunt	Revelation 3:20
The Four Horsemen of the Apocalypse	Dürer	Revelation 6:1-8; Zechariah 1:8-17, 6:12-17
The Great Day of His Wrath	John Martin	Revelation 6:12-17
Christ in Glory in the Tetramorph	Graham Sutherland	Revelation 4:1-11

Author's Acknowledgements

I'M GRATEFUL to Heather Prescott, Winifred Stone and Marian Allmark for their expert and often delightfully critical comments. I have made my own choices in the final analysis but hope they can see I have not been wholly deaf to their advice. Thanks also to Sarah, my daughter, who did so much early research for me, to the rest of the family for being ready sometimes to leave me alone to my own devices and sometimes to try out proposed text and pictures; and to my mother, Carol and Edna for processing the text.

Thanks are also due, though he doesn't realise it, to John V. Taylor, the former Bishop of Winchester. In his book, *The Go Between God*, are some works of art about which the author wrote: "I hope the reader may often turn to them – for they say it all better than I can hope to." This book and this particular comment began to transform my understanding of theology and of the way the Christian faith is understood and communicated. It is not a very big step from that book to this, although it is a timespan of many years.

Tony Cantale conceived the idea for the book and it has been a delight to work alongside him. Only he will know quite how challenging the search for the originals of some of the pictures really was.

There has been a wealth of background reading material used in preparing this work. I have always had beside me the Bible and commentaries on particular works of art, artists or galleries.

Two introductory companions that have been especially useful are *The Thames and Hudson Dictionary of Art and Artists*, London, Ed. Herbert Reed, Thames and Hudson 1994 and *The Oxford Companion to Christian Art and Architecture* by Peter and Linda Murray, OUP 1996. *The Christian Faith in Art* by Eric Newton and William Neil, Hodder, 1966, has been a valuable resource, and *The Story of Art* by E.H. Gombrich, Phaidon, 1989, was as sensitive in my chosen area as in so many others.

Keith J. White